Acadia Studies in Bible and Theology

Craig A. Evans and Lee Martin McDonald, General Editors

The last two decades have witnessed dramatic developments in biblical and theological study. Full-time academics can scarcely keep up with fresh discoveries, recently published primary texts, ongoing archaeological work, new exegetical proposals, experiments in methods and hermeneutics, and innovative theological syntheses. For students and nonspecialists these developments are confusing and daunting. What has been needed is a series of succinct studies that assess these issues and present their findings in a way that students, pastors, laity, and nonspecialists will find accessible and rewarding. Acadia Studies in Bible and Theology, sponsored by Acadia Divinity College in Wolfville, Nova Scotia, and in conjunction with the college's Hayward Lectureship, constitutes such a series.

The Hayward Lectureship has brought to Acadia many distinguished scholars of Bible and theology, such as Sir Robin Barbour, John Bright, Leander Keck, Helmut Koester, Richard Longenecker, Martin Marty, Jaroslav Pelikan, Ian Rennie, James Sanders, and Eduard Schweizer. Acadia Studies in Bible and Theology reflect this rich heritage.

These studies are designed to guide readers through the ever more complicated maze of critical, interpretative, and theological discussion taking place today. But these studies are not introductory in nature; nor are they mere surveys. Written by leading authorities in the field, Acadia Studies in Bible and Theology offer critical assessments of the major issues that the church faces in the twenty-first century. Readers will gain the requisite orientation and fresh understanding of the important issues that will enable them to take part meaningfully in discussion and debate.

BEYOND
the Bible

MOVING FROM
SCRIPTURE TO THEOLOGY

I. HOWARD MARSHALL

WITH ESSAYS BY KEVIN J. VANHOOZER
AND STANLEY E. PORTER

Baker Academic
Grand Rapids, Michigan

PATERNOSTER

© 2004 by I. Howard Marshall

Published by Baker Academic
a division of Baker Publishing Group
P.O. Box 6287, Grand Rapids, MI 49516-6287
www.bakeracademic.com

and

Paternoster
an imprint of Authentic Media
9 Holdom Avenue, Milton Keynes, Bucks., MK1 1QR UK
www.authenticmedia.co.uk

Printed in the United States of America

Library of Congress Cataloging-in-Publication Data
Marshall, I. Howard.
  Beyond the Bible : moving from scripture to theology / I. Howard Marshall ; with essays by Kevin J. Vanhoozer and Stanley E. Porter.
    p.   cm.—(Acadia studies in Bible and theology)
  Includes bibliographical references and index.
  ISBN 0-8010-2775-6 (pbk.)
  1. Bible. N.T.—Hermeneutics. 2. Bible. N.T.—Theology. 3. Dogma, Development of. 4. Theology, Doctrinal. I. Vanhoozer, Kevin J. II. Porter, Stanley E., 1956– III. Title. IV. Series.
BS2331.M27 2004
220.6′01—dc22   2004001766

British Library Cataloguing in Publication Data
A catalogue record for this book is available from the British Library.
Paternoster ISBN 1-84227-278-0

Contents

Preface

At a time when academic books are getting longer and longer and people have less and less time to read them, there may be a welcome for this comparatively short one that aims to set out an agenda for evangelical biblical scholarship.

The genesis of it lay in an invitation to me to give the annual lecture of the Institute for Biblical Research (IBR) at its annual meeting in Toronto in November 2002, and here I wish to express my thanks to Robert Gundry and the program committee for giving me that opportunity. One of the questions that was in my mind at the time of receiving the invitation was the impasse that has developed between scholars who come to different conclusions regarding issues such as the place of women in marriage and in ministry on the basis of different understandings of how the scriptural teaching, which they unite in accepting as authoritative, is to function today. Could there be any way of trying to understand what goes on in biblical interpretation and to see if there can be a *principled* way of moving from the ancient, authoritative text to its modern application? Greatly daring, I accepted the invitation and suggested the topic without being at all clear as to how it might be developed.

Then two further things happened. One was an invitation to write a chapter for a book to be entitled *The Futures of Evangelicalism* on "evangelicalism and biblical interpretation," setting out where we are at present and what ought to be our agenda for the future. The other was the invitation to deliver the series of three Hayward Lectures at Acadia Divinity College that came from Lee McDonald and Craig Evans, and again I wish to express my thanks to them and their colleagues and students both for the invitation and for the gracious reception and generous hospitality that I enjoyed in Wolfville. It seemed to me that the material that necessarily had to be given in a highly condensed form in the IBR lecture could helpfully be expanded for the Hayward Lectures, and also that some of the chapter for *The Futures of Evangelicalism* could be reproduced in this context as a lead-in to the topic, since the thesis of that chapter is quite simply that while we must continue to work at other aspects of biblical interpretation, the problem of how we are to get from the Bible to the church and the world today is the central task to which we must devote ourselves in the immediate future.

Craig Evans made the helpful suggestion that it would be good to have some kind of response to the lectures and took advantage of a visit by Stanley Porter to Acadia to get his insights on the theme. The only snag was that Stan's visit could take place only before the lecture series, and therefore the audience had the unusual—possibly unique—experience of hearing the response before the stimulus! However, the respondent was able to read an advance draft of my lectures before he spoke, and the chapter here that reproduces the substance of what he said has been revised in light of my final text. The reader of the present volume can now read the lectures and the response in the correct order!

Finally, it is customary for there to be an invited response to the IBR annual lecture, and this was given by Kevin Vanhoozer. I am indebted to both of my respondents for their contributions, which substantially further and expand the debate.

So you now have before you this brief symposium consisting of the Hayward Lectures and the papers by the two respondents. Both Stan and Kevin have made substantial contributions of their own to the discussion of hermeneutics, and what they have done in their chapters here is not so much to interact with the details of the lectures as to provide some stimulating supplementation on the basis of their own work. At the heart of Stan's chapter is a critical discussion of five different approaches to our problem: (1) an example of a historical-critical approach by

G. B. Caird; (2) an application of insights from L. Wittgenstein by A. C. Thiselton; (3) an application of speech-act theory used by both Thiselton and K. Vanhoozer; (4) the kind of developmental theory that is treated in my own discussion; and (5) an extension of the principle of dynamic equivalence from translation theory to interpretation by the author himself. There is perhaps rather more interaction with my proposals in the contribution by Kevin, and readers will be grateful to him (as I am) for drawing attention to debatable points and omissions in my treatment, but they will also appreciate the ways in which he draws out the different possible meanings of "going beyond Scripture."

I would make three brief comments here on the responses by Kevin and Stan. First, I am relieved that neither of my respondents has suggested that my approach is totally misguided and misleading, and I trust that this was not a matter of their native courtesy overcoming their better judgment. Second, it seems to me that many of the suggestions and approaches made by my colleagues are in no sense exclusive alternatives, and that in the complex art of interpretation a judicious combination of approaches and methods is essential. Third, it is good that students of the Bible and systematic theology have come together in this volume and appear to be not that far distant from each other; this strengthens my belief that what is being said here is essentially along the right lines.

I am encouraged, therefore, to believe that it is right to seek a principled way of moving from Scripture to its contemporary understanding and application, and that the way to do this is to explore how the principles can be established from Scripture itself, whether explicitly in terms of what the Bible itself has to say about how to understand the divine Word or implicitly in terms of how the biblical actors and writers actually understand the sources that were at their disposal. I have explored the way in which (as I see it) there is ongoing development of insight into God's revelation in Scripture, and I maintain that this process can provide us with guidelines for the ongoing and necessary task of apprehending what Scripture says and understanding and applying it in our own situation.

I. Howard Marshall

1

Evangelicals and Hermeneutics

O ver the past couple of decades I have encountered several students who wished to do research in the area of
hermeneutics. This represents one symptom of where we are in
biblical research at the present time. Hermeneutics is a central
concern in biblical studies. Galloping professional narrowness
will force me to deal here primarily with problems arising in the
area of the New Testament rather than in the Bible as a whole,
but what I have to say will, I hope, represent the position regarding evangelical biblical studies generally.

Sometimes it has seemed to me that students who expressed
this aim were not sure exactly what they really wanted to do,
whether to attempt some fresh approach to a biblical passage or
theme or to discuss broad principles of interpretation. I propose
to use the term "interpretation" to refer to the former activity of
interpreting the biblical text and to use the term "hermeneutics"
to refer to the science or art of interpretation; so "interpretation"

I am grateful to the editors and to Inter-Varsity Press for permission to use in this
chapter material that appeared in my contribution to C. Bartholomew, Robin
Parry, and Andrew West, eds., *The Futures of Evangelicalism: Issues and Prospects*
(Leicester: Inter-Varsity, 2003).

is what we do when we are actually dealing with the text, and "hermeneutics" is what we do when we discuss what is going on when we do interpretation. There is great uncertainty about this entire general area of hermeneutics and interpretation, not only in the narrower sector of biblical studies, but also in the broader field of literary studies and philosophy. Biblical interpretation, once perhaps almost taken for granted, has come to the fore as a disputed topic that demands scholarly attention.[1] It is not surprising that in this situation fresh attention has been paid to biblical interpretation within that branch of Christian faith and scholarship called "evangelical," and it is within this context that I wish to examine some key issues. My remarks, therefore, are addressed primarily to the evangelical constituency in the hope of helping us to put our own house in order, but I also hope that my observations will say something useful to all who are concerned to interpret the Bible for today.

The Importance of Evangelical Hermeneutics

Our topic is a broad one, and I will approach it from a particular angle that will help to focus our discussion. Hermeneutics is particularly important to us for two reasons. First, as Christian scholars who adhere to the evangelical faith, we are committed to *the academic study of Scripture* within a confessional framework, and therefore we must consider how this situation both liberates and constrains us as we carry out this task. But, second, as practicing Christians, we are also committed to *Christian witness in the contemporary world,* and therefore we need to ask questions about how we discover the message of the Bible for today, both for our fellow believers and for our non-Christian neighbors, and how we convey it to them. Clearly, these two commitments are interrelated, and it is increasingly recognized that they cannot be separated from one another. It is the latter task of expressing the

---

1. The current state of discussion is helpfully summarized in two solid dictionaries and a "companion": J. Barton, ed., *The Cambridge Companion to Biblical Interpretation* (Cambridge: Cambridge University Press, 1998); R. J. Coggins and J. L. Houlden, eds., *A Dictionary of Biblical Interpretation* (London: SCM; Philadelphia: Trinity, 1990); J. H. Hayes, ed., *Dictionary of Biblical Interpretation* (2 vols.; Nashville: Abingdon, 1991).

Christian message for today that will be our focus in this series. So in these three lectures I am particularly concerned with the question of how we use the Bible in our theology, ecclesiology, and ethics, but more especially in the first of these.[2] But first, it may be helpful to put the matter in a broader context.

Evangelicals share some problems of interpretation and hermeneutics with any other scholars or readers of texts as they attempt to understand what is being said; other problems arise from the fact that we are Christian believers, for whom the Bible is somehow different from other books, and we think rightly that the way in which we interpret it is or should be different.

What makes the Bible different from other books for us, of course, is that it is *Scripture,* which signifies (among other things) that it possesses authority over its readers, speaking in the language of truth and command. This alone, however, is not what makes the question of what the Bible says all the more important. If it is authoritative, we need to be as sure as possible about what it is that God says to us by way of promise and warning and what we are authoritatively called to believe and to do. Furthermore, there may be ways in which the process of interpretation is also different. If the Bible is a book that is in some sense authored by God, then an appropriate manner of interpretation is required. —➤ such a layered truth... God is orderly, logical, beyond understanding, mysterious, etc.

Three Levels of Study

The contemporary discussion of interpretation proceeds on three levels.

First, there is the level of *general hermeneutics,* which asks what is going on in interpretation in general and then in biblical interpretation in particular. Clearly, it is important to investigate hermeneutics at this level. I cite as examples two of the many vital questions that arise here. The first example is the question of whether texts can have "meaning" in themselves, meaning that is objectively there, so to speak, or whether meaning is

2. See K. J. Vanhoozer, "From Canon to Concept: 'Same' and 'Other' in the Relation between Biblical and Systematic Theology," *Scottish Bulletin of Evangelical Theology* 12 (1994): 96–124.

somehow created afresh through the interaction between the reader and the text, it being assumed that texts in themselves have no fixed meaning; clearly, this has considerable implications for our understanding of biblical authority.[3] The second example is the question of how language "works"[4]— how texts work, the roles of their authors and their readers, and so on. Study of these matters helps us to have some idea about what we may legitimately expect from different kinds of texts, how we should approach them, and what are the implications of this for recognizing what is actually going on in biblical texts and in our reading of them.[5] However, largely out of comparative ignorance of this area and also because it is perhaps less immediately fruitful for the nitty-gritty of biblical interpretation than the other two levels of study, I propose to leave it to one side.

Second, there is the level of *exegesis*. Here we consider the specific procedures that may be applied to textual study, such as linguistic study, contextual study, source criticism, and much else. These methods and tools are used in approaching a text so as to understand it as it was understood or was meant to be understood in its own time.

Third, there is the level of *exposition* or *application*, where we raise the question of how to determine what an ancient text is saying to contemporary readers as opposed to original readers. Even if, say, Luke or Paul understood themselves to be writing "Scripture" in the sense of works meant for Christians everywhere for the foreseeable future,[6] they did so within the

3. K. J. Vanhoozer, *Is There a Meaning in This Text? The Bible, the Reader, and the Morality of Literary Knowledge* (Grand Rapids: Zondervan, 1998).

4. One example of this is the question of what a lexicon or dictionary of New Testament Greek should provide and how it should be organized.

5. See especially C. Bartholomew, C. Greene, and K. Möller, eds., *Renewing Biblical Interpretation* (Scripture and Hermeneutics 1; Carlisle: Paternoster; Grand Rapids: Zondervan, 2000).

6. In my view, an apostle, writing as an apostle, claimed authority for his writings and believed that they were authoritative not just for the specific audience and occasion, but also more widely. In some cases it seems that the writers were conscious of producing something akin to Scripture: the way in which Luke deliberately used septuagintal language and forms may suggest that he was conscious of carrying on an uncompleted story; the appeal by Paul in several of his letters to his status as apostle and/or slave of Christ may indicate that he was conscious of writing with the authority appropriate to a delegate of

to a certain degree they did
i.e. typology!

boundaries of their particular world and did not foresee the world of which we are part, and therefore there is a legitimate and necessary question about how their works can continue to function as Scripture for us.

These three levels of discussion are inextricably bound together. The classic modern example of the interrelatedness comes perhaps in the person of R. Bultmann, who read the New Testament in light of the philosophy of M. Heidegger, so that to some extent a demythologized version of its teaching emerges even in his *New Testament Theology*. Bultmann, in other words, was to some extent setting out what he thought Christians ought to believe today rather than simply describing the theology of the New Testament on its own terms.[7]

The Development of Evangelical Biblical Interpretation

Until comparatively recently evangelicals, like biblical scholars and preachers generally, did not recognize how great are the problems in these three areas. Of course, handbooks of biblical interpretation were available. In my student days, for example, Alan M. Stibbs wrote three booklets at a fairly nontechnical level, one of which was called *Understanding God's Word*. Some of us jokingly suggested at the time that Stibbs might also have written a book on liberal interpretation of the Bible to be called *Misunderstanding God's Word*. That was a characteristic example of juvenile conceit and a typical triumphalist evangelical claim that we alone are right.

Nevertheless, there was a growing awareness of the need for deeper discussion. A single example must suffice. Thirty years ago we were no doubt influenced by the mood of the times when the

---

Christ, and there are similarities between him and the prophets (K. O. Sandnes, *Paul—One of the Prophets? A Contribution to the Apostle's Self-Understanding* [Wissenschaftliche Untersuchungen zum Neuen Testament 2.43; Tübingen: Mohr, 1991]); the writer of the book of Revelation specifically claimed to be writing what Christ told him to write, and he uttered a curse on anyone who added to or subtracted from his work.

7. R. Bultmann, *Theology of the New Testament* (2 vols.; London: SCM, 1953–1955), 2:237–51.

New Testament study group of the Tyndale Fellowship devoted its meeting in 1973 to the topic and discussed a set of papers that eventually were published in 1977 under the title *New Testament Interpretation: Essays on Principles and Methods*. The book was intended to be a comprehensive introductory textbook for theological students. In his essay "Approaches to New Testament Exegesis" in that book, R. P. Martin commended what he termed "the grammatico-historical method." He contrasted it with what he called "the dogmatic approach" and "the impressionistic approach." The former approach viewed Scripture as a series of theological proof-texts, often interpreted in light of later ecclesiastical statements, while the latter worked more with the "blessed thoughts" that a passage of Scripture excited in the minds of the readers. It is fair to say that at a popular level these kinds of interpretation were used often. By contrast, "the grammatico-historical method" takes seriously the fact that the Bible is a book from a particular historical setting and consists of words in the original languages; genuine interpretation must take account of the setting and attempt to understand the text using all possible resources that will explain the wording. Scripture must be understood on its own terms.[8]

In commending the "*grammatico*-historical method," Martin probably also was distancing himself from the "historical-*critical* method," which was the dominant approach in biblical scholarship. These two terms sound very similar, and the latter method used the same tools as the former. However, as formulated by scholars such as E. Troeltsch, the historical-critical method was based on a denial of the supernatural and attempted to understand the biblical text as simply a human, fallible collection of documents. As a consequence, historical criticism in the broad sense was viewed with disfavor by evangelicals; they believed that its presuppositions were invalid and therefore that its conclusions must be false, and so they were tempted to reject it lock, stock, and barrel. Evangelicals were also wary of a method that seemed to work largely by discovering errors and contradictions in the Bible and building theories upon them. Underlying all of this was also the perception that this method was spiritually bar-

---

8. See R. P. Martin, "Approaches to New Testament Exegesis," in *New Testament Interpretation: Essays on Principles and Methods* (ed. I. H. Marshall; Exeter: Paternoster, 1977), 220–51.

ren because it seemed to be more concerned with exploring how texts came into existence than with elucidating their theological significance. Students walked out of theological seminaries with the feeling that they had learned very little that would help them to preach from Scripture.

To cite a favorite example, the documentary theory about the origins of the Pentateuch was regarded with disfavor because: (1) it denied the Mosaic authorship of Genesis (which was assumed to be asserted in the Bible [e.g., John 1:45]); (2) to a considerable extent it based the dissection of the narrative into sections from different sources on the exposure of discrepancies and contradictions between different texts; and (3) it tended to ignore the divine authority of the text. Thus, serious questions arose about what the documentary theory did in trying to explain the biblical text in terms of its sources and the influences upon its writers in such a way that its claim to be in some way based upon revelation was disputed. More recent criticism of it (not just by evangelicals) has also claimed that in principle the method could not bring out the message of the Bible for today. Maybe the reason for this was that it did not really try to do so and simply stopped short of asking what the text might mean for its readers as Scripture. Yet a great deal of biblical study was conducted in this manner.

Faced by the prevalence of this approach, evangelicals reacted in two ways.

First, a few scholars attempted to deal with such problems by taking on the critics on their own ground, producing reasoned refutations of their theories and attempting to frame better ones. Among scholars who did so we might mention G. Ch. Aalders, whose *Short Introduction to the Pentateuch* kept me going during my student days, G. T. Manley, author of *The Book of the Law*, and, towering above them all on the New Testament side, J. G. Machen, whose *Virgin Birth of Christ* came to my rescue after a series of seminars in Germany back in 1959.[9] The point to be emphasized is that whether or not these evangelical scholars were right in their historical conclusions, they recognized the

9. G. Ch. Aalders, *A Short Introduction to the Pentateuch* (London: Tyndale, 1949); G. T. Manley, *The Book of the Law: Studies in the Date of Deuteronomy* (London: Tyndale, 1957); J. G. Machen, *The Virgin Birth of Christ* (1930; repr., London: James Clarke, 1958).

need for scholarly historical study of the issues. The questions asked by the critics were legitimate and demanded answers.

Second, probably the majority of evangelicals simply took refuge in their belief in scriptural infallibility, claiming that whatever critics might say, the biblical statements about authorship and forecasts made in predictive prophecies were, by definition, historically infallible. Many interpreters, therefore, simply ignored the "higher critics" (as they called them) and their conclusions. There was a consequent distrust of scholarship of any kind. For a long time, very little serious evangelical scholarship was undertaken, and evangelical candidates for ministry sometimes were counseled by their elders to avoid pursuing theological degrees lest they be infected with higher criticism and lose their faith.

As for actual interpretation of the text, evangelical scholars followed the practices of the time. Essentially, exegesis was carried on perfectly properly by linguistic and syntactical study to discover what the text was saying. Background information was drawn upon to explain it. There was, however, a tendency to focus on elucidating the details of the text verse by verse rather than to look at larger units of text and their total thrust. For those of us who were students at the time, the publication of the Tyndale New Testament Commentaries series was an absolute Godsend, but even then I was sadly aware that in some cases insufficient attention was paid to the structure of the biblical books and to the elucidation of their theology.

It was then assumed that the text would speak to the modern reader more or less as it stood. There was, therefore, little need for "interpretation" in the sense of reapplying the text to different circumstances or translating it to make it intelligible to people who did not stand in the original situation. For the most part it could be assumed that there was little or no difference between the original readers and the contemporary readers. It may be significant that even in my 1977 symposium only one out of eighteen essays was directly concerned with the question of how one expounds the text for the modern reader.[10]

We thus have a situation in which there was little or no scholarship (despite the exceptions already noted), evangelicalism was

10. Three other essays did look at related topics.

largely defensive, and hermeneutics was not seen as a problem. It is fair to say that at the center of whatever discussion did take place were the questions of authorship and historicity, since these issues were most germane to the authenticity and authority of the biblical texts.

But then came several books like the one generated by the aforementioned symposium. What caused the change? Over the past fifty years or so remarkable growth has occurred in the industry of biblical scholarship on all sides, and in particular tremendous interest has arisen in "hermeneutics" or "interpretation" in the broadest sense by scholars of all persuasions. Also, some welcome shifts in scholarship have taken place, three of which are of particular significance.

First, there has been a recognition that all the biblical books are, in different degrees, *theological documents,* and that one of the main aims, if not the main aim, of interpretation should be to elucidate their theology. A number of major series of commentaries have made this their explicit aim. Once this fact is admitted, it follows that attention is concentrated on the message of the Bible.

Second, at the same time there has been a recognition that texts should be studied in their own right as *literary entities.* This has led to a concentration of attention on the texts in their final forms and to a lessened interest in how they came to be. For example, earlier studies of Matthew and Luke tended to look at them redactionally, asking how the authors used their sources. Now, however, the current impasse in solving the Synoptic problem has prompted a shift to asking how the evangelists have told their stories, and narrative criticism and discourse analysis have begun to eclipse source criticism and redaction criticism.[11] Most of the recent developments in new approaches to the text tend to be what we might call literary approaches as opposed to historical approaches.

Third, there has also developed the discipline of *canonical criticism,* which insists that books be interpreted not only in their final form, but also as part of a canonical collection of

11. It is important to stress that the older disciplines by no means have disappeared from use; they remain important, but other disciplines tend to occupy the center of attention.

Scripture, and this has led us back to something rather like the old principle of "interpreting Scripture by Scripture."

These three developments mean that biblical scholarship in general is concentrating on areas that are more congenial to evangelicals.

We are inevitably influenced by our context, and the development of evangelical biblical scholarship over this period must be understood, at least to some extent, against this broader background of a more positive approach.

Alongside these developments in scholarship at large that have been congenial to evangelical study of the New Testament, a shift also has taken place within evangelicalism. This is the recognition on the part of many, but not all, scholars that the methods of critical study can be used without acceptance of antireligious presuppositions that rule out the possibility of the supernatural from the start. It is possible to do "grammatico-historical" study without accepting the starting point laid down by Troeltsch.[12] Over against the skeptical "historical-critical method" may be placed the approach of "believing criticism."[13]

I must comment in passing that this has led to some diversity in critical stances, although this is not a new phenomenon. In the 1940s there took place the creation of the Tyndale Fellowship, which was a serious attempt to develop an evangelical scholarship that could face up to the challenges of biblical criticism honestly and fairly. Writing in 1947, one of its leading founder members, F. F. Bruce, contrasted the attitude at that time of the Roman Catholic Church, which fettered its scholars, to that of the Tyndale Fellowship:

> In such critical *cruces*, for example, as the codification of the Pentateuch, the composition of Isaiah, the date of Daniel, the sources

12. See W. J. Abraham, *Divine Revelation and the Limits of Historical Criticism* (Oxford: Oxford University Press, 1982).

13. D. F. Wright, in "Soundings in the Doctrine of Scripture in British Evangelicalism in the First Half of the Twentieth Century" (*Tyndale Bulletin* 31 [1980]: 87–106), mentions J. K. Mozley using this term to describe a rather wider range of scholarship. (I am grateful to an unpublished thesis by S. P. Dray for this reference.) I use the term to designate an approach that recognizes that the manner of the human composition of the biblical books is a proper subject for investigation by scholars who also believe in their divine origin and inspiration.

of the Gospels, or the authenticity of the Pastoral Epistles, each of us is free to hold and proclaim the conclusions to which all the available evidence points. Any research worthy of the name, we take it for granted, must necessarily be unfettered.[14]

It must be admitted that Bruce's statement represented the ideal rather than what was always the reality. Evangelical publishers in particular have not always been willing to publish authorial views inconsistent with their own or those of their constituency for fear of the very real possibility of losing their clientele. Here we might note the fierce reaction to proposed revisions to the New International Version from those who feared that it would lend support to egalitarian views of the place of women in the home and the ministry, which led to the American Bible Society retracting from its intentions.[15] It is evident that the problems of pressure from people with clout on publishers and of censorship by publishers themselves have not gone away.[16]

To some extent, then, in much recent study a rapprochement has come about between scholars in conservative camps and those in liberal camps, with a recognition that each group may have something to learn from the other. This has taken place because the more recent study of biblical texts has tended to be conducted on the level of texts as literary objects rather than that of texts as witnesses to historical events, and this type of study does not raise the questions of historicity, sources, and so on that formed a major battleground in the past.[17]

14. F. F. Bruce, "The Tyndale Fellowship for Biblical Research," *Evangelical Quarterly* 19 (1947): 58–59. In a footnote Bruce noted how *Evangelical Quarterly* had carried contributions that expressed different views on the common authorship of the Gospel of John and the book of Revelation by George Beasley-Murray and himself.

15. The solution, worthy of Solomon, adopted by the publishers is to continue to publish the unrevised NIV to satisfy one part of the constituency and to publish a revised version under a different name, Today's New International Version, for the benefit of the other part. (Presumably, this was not meant to imply that those sticking to the NIV have embraced yesterday's version.)

16. It is vital that evangelical scholars be able to publish views that are novel and even questionable so that they can be openly discussed by their peers without the proponents being censored or drummed out of the corps.

17. The problems are still very real, however, in Old Testament scholarship, where the so-called Copenhagen School wants to deny the historicity of most of the narrative.

There are, of course, dangers in conducting literary study apart from historical study. One is the temptation to explain the texts purely on the literary level. I recall, for example, one attempt to explain Luke's portrayal of women in the early church simply in terms of his particular motivation rather than recognizing that he was constrained by the historical phenomena that he was describing. Evangelicals have an important role to play here in stressing the relation of the texts to the historical events that underlie them. There also exists the temptation to ignore the thorny historical questions in order to focus on less controversial issues. At present, for example, much less attention is being paid to the questions of the sources of the books of the Old Testament, and preference is being given to the study of those books as completed wholes (however they may have reached that state). Certainly, this emphasis on the final form of the text is to be welcomed; nevertheless, the question of history cannot be sidestepped forever. And evangelicals would want to insist that if the text does not witness to a genuine saving and judging intervention of God in human history, then "we are of all men most miserable."[18]

From these considerations, we might surmise that evangelical scholars are more open to the scholarly study of the text using whatever scholarly tools are available, even if this means that there is less unanimity on issues of authorship and historicity.

Current Issues in Evangelical Scholarship

In light of these remarks, we may now briefly examine the state of scholarship at the present time, doing so in terms of the three levels of discussion outlined above.

General Hermeneutics

Evangelical scholars have both welcomed and advanced the developments in general hermeneutics that have been taking

18. In making this allusion to 1 Cor. 15:19, I ask the reader to permit me to use the inclusive sense of "men" current when the version I am citing (AV/KJV) was penned.

place in recent years. Some of the most important contributions to the discussion in this area have been made by R. Lundin, A. C. Thiselton, and K. Vanhoozer, and these have attracted wide attention. A wider discussion, led by Craig Bartholomew and involving scholars from a variety of theological positions, is taking place in the "Scripture and Hermeneutics Seminar."[19]

Exegesis

Here it is interesting to compare two textbooks for students coming out of the evangelical stable. The book that I edited twenty-five years ago covered, among other things, semantics, introduction (authorship, audience, date, etc.), religious background, historical criticism, source criticism, form criticism, tradition history, redaction criticism, genre,[20] and use of the Old Testament. Exegesis was covered by an article that looked at two difficult passages and explored how to go about understanding them, while another article on exposition looked at the same passages and how to draw significance out of them for today. All of these approaches were recognized as legitimate, necessary, and valuable for understanding the text.

Over against this we may place the much more recent book *Hearing the New Testament: Strategies for Interpretation*. Its list of topics includes traditio-historical criticism* (the asterisks in this list mark the topics common to both volumes in order to indicate the degree of overlap between them); historical criticism and social-scientific perspectives; the relevance of extracanonical Jewish texts; the relevance of Greco-Roman literature and culture; textual criticism; modern linguistics*; discourse analy-

19. At the time of this writing, three volumes of papers and responses have appeared: C. Bartholomew, C. Greene, and K. Möller, eds., *Renewing Biblical Interpretation* (Scripture and Hermeneutics 1; Carlisle: Paternoster; Grand Rapids: Zondervan, 2000); idem, eds., *After Pentecost: Language and Biblical Interpretation* (Scripture and Hermeneutics 2; Carlisle: Paternoster; Grand Rapids: Zondervan, 2001); C. Bartholomew et al., eds., *A Royal Priesthood? The Use of the Bible Ethically and Politically: A Dialogue with Oliver O'Donovan* (Scripture and Hermeneutics 3; Carlisle: Paternoster; Grand Rapids: Zondervan, 2002). The Seminar is conducted under the auspices of the University of Gloucestershire's School of Theology and Religious Studies and the British and Foreign Bible Society.

20. This was covered in Martin, "Approaches to New Testament Exegesis" (see note 8 above), which explored the different types of material in the letters.

sis; genre analysis*; the use of the Old Testament*; narrative criticism; rhetorical criticism; the place of the reader in New Testament interpretation; feminist hermeneutics; and reading the New Testament in canonical context.[21] Three things here merit further discussion.

First, there is the number of approaches to New Testament study that were only beginning to be heard of in 1977 or that had not developed sufficiently to be thought worthy of mention.[22] Thus, although there has always been recognition of the need to study the Jewish and non-Jewish texts of the period in order to shed fuller light on the New Testament, new tools (e.g., computerized texts and search procedures) and new discoveries (e.g., the availability of the full corpus of the Dead Sea Scrolls) have revolutionized this area. But there are also new types of analysis of the text, such as discourse analysis, rhetorical criticism, and reader-response criticism, which have come to the fore and made us ask new questions of the text. I wish to emphasize that all such questioning is legitimate, provided that it is not driven by the motive of discrediting the text and not regarded as the key to solving all our problems.

Second is the fact that evangelical scholars not only have taken up these approaches, but also in a number of cases have made important contributions to their development. A few examples may be mentioned here. Representative of the more traditional approaches is the outstanding work of B. M. Metzger in establishing the text of the Greek New Testament. The pioneer work of E. A. Judge in developing a social-scientific approach to the New Testament is widely esteemed. Some of the most important work in the study of Greek syntax has been carried out by S. E. Porter, B. Fanning, and D. B. Wallace.[23] The work of J. B. Green in developing a literary approach to the study of the Gospel of Luke has been very favorably received by many reviewers. "Here

21. J. B. Green, ed., *Hearing the New Testament: Strategies for Interpretation* (Carlisle: Paternoster; Grand Rapids: Eerdmans, 1995).

22. One regrettable omission in the 1977 book was textual criticism.

23. S. E. Porter, *Verbal Aspect in the Greek of the New Testament, with Reference to Tense and Mood* (Studies in Biblical Greek 1; New York: Lang, 1989); B. M. Fanning, *Verbal Aspect in New Testament Greek* (Oxford Theological Monographs; Oxford: Clarendon, 1990); D. B. Wallace, *Greek Grammar Beyond the Basics: An Exegetical Syntax of the New Testament* (Grand Rapids: Zondervan, 1996).

at last," says Gordon Fee, general editor of the series in which Green's volume appears, "is a commentary on Luke that tries to help the reader to see how the narrative 'works.'"[24] Several of the contributors to Green's *Hearing the New Testament* are making their mark as frontrunners in new approaches.

Third, the fruits of this study are seen in the commentaries being produced by evangelical scholars. Series such as the New International Commentary on the New Testament, the New International Greek Testament Commentary, the Word Biblical Commentary, and the Pillar New Testament Commentary bear testimony to the level of activity at the present time. Thus, at the level of exegesis of the text, evangelical scholars are playing an important role in the development and the application of methods of study.

Work of this kind is based on the axiom that all interpretation of the text must begin with the attempt to understand it as clearly as possible in terms of its original setting. There is much debate as to whether such a thing as unbiased exegesis can exist or whether all of us are unconsciously affected by the presuppositions that we bring to the study of the text. Perhaps in principle it is impossible for modern readers to discover what Mark was trying to say or what his first-century readers would have gotten out of his text, but I am not so pessimistic about this. The point about the impossibility of presuppositionless exegesis must be conceded; nevertheless, its significance is easily exaggerated. We must beware of a fallacious argument that says that if one cannot draw an exact boundary at every point, then the boundary either cannot be traced or does not exist at all. Granted that absolute objectivity is impossible to achieve, it simply does not follow that a relative objectivity must be unattainable. In fact, exegetes come out of many different cultures and times, and when there is agreement among them on the methods to be employed and, to a considerable extent, on the conclusions that are reached, then we may be reasonably sure that we are within sight of a valid exegesis.

Some areas are, obviously, more factual than others. I contend that in the spheres of Greek lexicography and grammar we

---

24. J. B. Green, *The Gospel of Luke* (New International Commentary on the New Testament; Grand Rapids: Eerdmans, 1997), vii.

have a very solid basis indeed of reasonably certain knowledge. More controversially, I claim the same for reconstruction of the original text of the Greek New Testament. And many aspects of the actual interpretation of the text are generally agreed upon, even though commentators continue to argue and debate with one another.

We have, therefore, a fairly sound starting point for the third part of the task of interpretation, to which I now turn.

Exposition or Application

Possibly the most important and controversial issue to be considered is that of the exposition or application of the text. How do we read and appropriate ancient texts in the contemporary world?

For a typical answer we may turn to J. I. Packer. In an essay entitled "Understanding the Bible: Evangelical Hermeneutics,"[25] originally published in 1990, he begins by stressing the distinctive character of evangelical hermeneutics on the basis that "evangelicals say that they should listen to Holy Scripture, and finally let its teaching guide them, however much reordering of their prior ideas and intentions this may involve, and however sharply it may set them at odds with the mind-set of their peers and their times."[26]

He then states four principles that govern their interpretation:

1. "Biblical passages must be taken to mean *what their human authors were consciously expressing.*" For what the human authors say is what God says.[27]
2. "The *coherence, harmony and veracity* of all biblical teaching must be taken as our working hypothesis in interpretation."[28]

25. J. I. Packer, "Understanding the Bible: Evangelical Hermeneutics," in *Honouring the Written Word of God* (vol. 3 of *The Collected Shorter Writings of J. I. Packer;* Carlisle: Paternoster, 1999), 147–60.
26. Ibid., 150.
27. Ibid., 153.
28. Ibid., 155.

3. "Interpretation involves *synthesizing* what the various biblical passages teach, so that each item taught finds its proper place and significance in the *organism* of revelation as a whole." Under this heading Packer comments that progressive revelation "is not an evolutionary process of growing spiritual discernment through which cruder notions come to be left behind," but rather "earlier revelation became the foundation for later revelation."[29]

4. *"The response for which the text calls* must be made explicit." Here the crucial procedure appears:

> So, just as it is possible to identify in all the books of Scripture universal and abiding truths about the will, work and ways of God, it is equally possible to find in every one of them universal and abiding principles of loyalty and devotion to the holy, gracious Creator; and then to detach these from the particular situations to which, and the cultural frames within which, the books apply them, and to reapply them to ourselves in the places, circumstances, and conditions of our own lives today. Rational application of this kind, acknowledging but transcending cultural differences between the Bible worlds and ours, is the stock-in-trade of the evangelical pulpit, and the recognized goal of the evangelical discipline of personal meditation on the written text. . . . Evangelicals do not find their models of interpretation in the "critical" commentaries of the last century and a half, which stop short at offering historical explanations of the text and have no applicatory angle at all; they find them, rather, in the from-faith-to-faith expository styles of . . . older writers . . . who concerned themselves with what Scripture means as God's word to their own readers, as well as with what it meant as religious instruction for the readership originally addressed, and whose supreme skill lay in making appropriate applications of the material that they exegeted by grammatico-historical means.[30]

Similar statements might have been taken from several sources,[31] for what Packer says here is representative of an agreed position. He makes a distinction between what we may

---

29. Ibid., 155–56.
30. Ibid., 157.
31. In a popular magazine, Jack Kuhatschek writes this:
   To apply most New Testament commands, we need to understand the

call statements of doctrine and principles of response to God. The former, it seems, are accepted as they stand. However, it is recognized that the forms in which the latter are presented may be shaped by particular situations ("Go to the great city of Nineveh and preach against it" [Jon. 1:2]) and cultural frameworks ("Let people and animals be covered with sackcloth. Let everyone call urgently on God" [Jon. 3:8]), and we are required to detach the principles of response to God's message and then make a rational reapplication of them to ourselves in our situation and cultural setting.

We thus have a hermeneutical procedure that commands fairly wide assent and is common practice. However, it cannot be said to solve all our problems. Here, three points may be made.

First, this hermeneutical procedure does not always lead to the same results even among interpreters who may be presumed to be living in much the same kind of setting. Fifty years ago there was virtual unanimity among evangelicals in confining the ordained ministry and church leadership to men, but today such agreement no longer exists. The practice of apartheid, which was based on a particular understanding of Scripture by Christians who professed to be "Reformed," has come to be recognized as incompatible with scriptural teaching. On matters of doctrine there are important questions regarding the nature of justice and judgment and, consequently, regarding the understanding of the atonement.[32] Whereas evangelicals tended to adopt in practice a supersessionist understanding of certain gifts of the Spirit (espe-

---

original situation. If the situation is identical or comparable to our own situation, then we can apply the command directly to our lives.

If not, then we need to discover the principle behind the command and apply it to comparable situations that we face.

With some New Testament commands we don't need to find general principles for the specific situations. Rather, we need to find specific situations for the general principles. [e.g., applying love command]

The list is virtually endless. But we haven't applied the commands of Scripture until we have thought about what we could do, ask God for wisdom and guidance, and then act on His guidance ("Applying Scripture," *Decision* 42, no. 9 [September 2001]: 47).

32. The questions concern the nature of human punishment. Should it be retributive as well as deterrent and reformatory? How is it related to the divine judgment upon sin, and should the latter be understood as primarily retribu-

cially speaking in tongues, prophecy, and healing), there has been a revival of these gifts in charismatic congregations accompanied by a reappraisal of the doctrine of the Holy Spirit.

Second, a further set of problems arises where the Christian is called upon to deal with contemporary issues to which there is nothing closely analogous in Scripture (or in the ancient world generally). Typically, these are issues raised by modern scientific and medical technology, such as questions of fertilization, contraception, genetic modification, and termination of life. How is Scripture to be utilized in these areas?[33] A preaching ministry that always starts from Scripture and expounds the text is in danger of never reaching such problems, the solutions to which may depend upon the thrust of Scripture as a whole rather than upon a single passage.

Third, yet another area arises with more general issues of human life, as when Christians would campaign against slavery or unrepresentative government although these are not questioned in Scripture and people apparently are encouraged to live obediently within such social and political frameworks and are never urged to campaign toward fundamental changes in the structures of society and state (the principle of obeying "God rather than human beings" [Acts 5:29] appears to apply only where human authorities forbid Christian witness). How do Christians justify civil rights movements, peaceful protests, acts of civil disobedience, and the like?

Thus, a broad range of questions emerges where adoption of this hermeneutical "method" does not necessarily lead to unanimity in interpretation. Problems arise at the levels of exegesis of individual texts, constructing a synthesis or harmony of biblical teaching, and making a relevant application of the biblical teaching. It is not surprising, therefore, that evangelicals (like other Christians) are examining afresh the ways in which we can appropriate the message of Scripture for ourselves, or, better, to find out how we can discern what God is telling us through

---

tive? See C. D. Marshall, *Beyond Retribution: A New Testament Vision for Justice* (Grand Rapids: Eerdmans, 2001).

33. See, for example, G. Jones, *Clones: The Clowns of Technology?* (Carlisle: Paternoster, 2001); D. Bruce and D. Horrocks, eds., *Modifying Creation? GM Crops and Foods: A Christian Perspective* (Carlisle: Paternoster, 2001).

Scripture to believe and do. Moreover, these problems are concerned not only with the application of principles, but also in some cases with the status of the principles themselves.

There are also some problems about the method itself, of which I will mention four.

First, although Packer's approach clearly is designed to outlaw various untenable forms of allegorical interpretation, it is not clear that the stress on what the *human* writers intended to express can do justice to what is commonly called the *sensus plenior*, the fuller sense that texts may have as a result of their divine inspiration or their place in the wider history of salvation and the development of the canon. Thus, for example, 1 Pet. 1:10–12 suggests that writers may have written texts that contained more than they themselves could understand because the reference of prophecy was not always clear to them.

Second, although the assumption that Scripture is the Word of God and therefore truthful is crucial for evangelicals, it cannot be postulated in advance what this assumption means in detail. Does it, for example, mean that a story that appears to us to be told as if it is a narrative of what actually happened is a historical account in the sense that every detail occurred exactly as it is related? What about the story of Jonah, which perhaps is a short story making important theological points rather than a historical account? And when it is said that the biblical account as a whole is coherent, harmonious, and veracious, is this true at the surface level or perhaps only at a deeper level? In what ways are apparent contradictions to be resolved?

Third, problems also arise where teaching is given, particularly in the Old Testament, that seems more like "cruder notions" to be abandoned than "the foundation for later revelation." The divine approval (expressed or tacit) of genocide in certain situations is an obvious and disturbing example.

Fourth, I find no problem in the important statement that the interpretation of Scripture is meant to lead to a response from the readers, but more needs to be said about what kinds of responses are required.[34]

---

34. I do not wish to give the false impression that Packer has not tackled these questions more fully elsewhere, but even so, I am sure that he would agree that he has not put these issues to rest and that we must continue to debate them.

All this shows that we cannot assume that the last word has been spoken on the matter, but rather that we must look at this question of understanding and application in a fresh way. So what I wish to do is to open up the question of how we get from the Bible to Christian doctrine and practice in the contemporary world, or how we get back to the Bible from our contemporary questions and problems in the areas of belief and behavior.

Let me conclude this first installment of my remarks by noting two unacceptable ways of proceeding.

First, evangelicals generally are clear that they should not go down the path of classical "liberalism," by which is meant the peeling off of those aspects of biblical teaching about Christian faith and ethics that are held by many people today to be incompatible with a so-called scientific worldview and an "enlightened" understanding of morality. Although we would argue strongly that to do so is to make a secular understanding the lens for reading Scripture, we should nevertheless try to understand sympathetically what motivates the liberal approach, and I shall want to return later to the challenge with which it confronts us.

Second, we should not travel the route of "fundamentalism," although it may not be so clear to some evangelicals why this is so. One of the results of the surge of contemporary fundamentalisms in different types of religion and even in politics has been a closer scrutiny of the nature of the phenomenon. It has been shown that in many cases what is going on is not simply the appeal to an authoritative text whose interpretation lies beyond question, but rather the buttressing of the authority of a human leader or leaders who so identify themselves with a policy that they justify from the sacred text that any challenge to their authority can be treated as a challenge to the authority of the text. In many cases we would observe that what is being upheld is not only the infallibility of an ancient text, but also the infallibility of a particular tradition of interpretation that is proffered as authoritative and beyond question. But in fact the interpretation is usually just one possibility, often a superficially obvious and attractive one to its supporters, and the text is being used as an instrument to force obedience to the human authority. So, for example, the *Sharia* law is but one interpretation of the Koran, but within certain sects of Islam to disagree with it is to disagree with the ayatollahs. We need, therefore, to ask whether sometimes—I don't say always—fundamentalism is a defense of a postbiblical traditional interpretation rather than a willingness to go back to the text and to be led by it.

In place of these two extremes we need an interpretation of the Bible that is determined by the Bible itself—if such a thing is possible. Therefore, I propose that we look for ways of interpreting the Bible that are themselves biblical. What I wish to do in the two remaining lectures is to make a start in asking whether such a thing is possible, and if so, what it might look like.

2

The Development
of Doctrine

In the first of these lectures I have been concerned to show
how hermeneutics has become a major problem within biblical scholarship at the present time and to say something about
how this has affected evangelical study of the New Testament
in particular. I established that there is an ongoing discussion
of general hermeneutics and of methods of textual study, and I
argued that in the latter area there has been a growing consensus
that the aim of interpretation is to elucidate the theological message of the New Testament by making use of historical and literary study. I then claimed that the major area that still requires
discussion is how we get from the Bible to the contemporary
world: how do we appropriate the message of the Bible so that
present-day readers may apply it to themselves and the problems
that they face? Until recently there was a tendency to see this
as a straightforward reading of the text that did no more than
make due allowances for the specificity of the biblical teaching
and generalize it to apply to people in different situations and
cultures. Unfortunately, we can no longer rest content with this
approach. The issues are more complicated.

Two Approaches to the Use of Scripture

I will attempt to make my point by looking at three areas of appropriation and demonstrating that we have two distinguishable approaches to the problems that arise. The boundary between them is fuzzy, and therefore it may be difficult to make a sufficiently sharp distinction between them; nevertheless, I think that two recognizably different trends in interpretation can be traced. For examples, we will look in turn at ethics, church order, and doctrine.

Two Approaches to Ethics

We start with *ethics*. On the one hand, we have what may be called the traditional approach, which says that the individual commands and exhortations in the Bible are to be taken at their face value unless there are strong reasons for not doing so. Two such reasons generally are adduced here.

First, the commands may have been given *in a specific situation* that is past and gone. Believers are no longer required to pray specifically for Paul as a missionary, but by analogy and generalization they should pray for contemporary missionaries.

Second, the commands may have been given in a form *appropriate to a particular cultural setting* but no longer appropriate in ours. Believers are no longer required to greet one another with a kiss, but they should greet one another in whatever way is fitting in their cultural or social setting.

Thus, we might say that for this approach the "plain" sense of Scripture is authoritative unless it is manifestly not universalizable. Further, such an approach will, in general, not go beyond Scripture except in the sense that individual commands are to be seen as particular examples of general principles whose application can be appropriately extended to cover different situations. Also, this approach tends to focus on specific passages and, while not ignoring the fact that Scripture must be interpreted in the light of Scripture, to pay less attention to the general thrust of scriptural teaching as a whole. This approach, then, sees Scripture as instantiating general principles of universal validity by expressing them in specific ways that may be tied to particular situations or cultural expressions.

On the other hand, there is the approach that holds that there may be cases where, for example, some scriptural teaching is relativized by other teaching, or where we are called to do things that may go beyond scriptural teaching.

Let us look at two examples of *relativization*. Few if any contemporary Christians would accept that it is permissible on any occasions to practice genocide, although apparently this was sometimes done at divine command in some circumstances (Josh. 11:14–15, 20). Again, most Christians would accept that although some biblical authors do not question the institution of slavery but rather give regulations for those within it, Christians today should not practice it. It is important to note that the reasons for not accepting genocide or slavery do not lie in any cultural shift, but arise out of a conviction that these practices are intrinsically wrong in view of broader biblical teaching.

And let us look at an example of *going beyond Scripture*. We might mention again the way in which Christians tend to be supporters of democracy over against oligarchy or despotism, and many Christians would work actively in politics to achieve democratic forms of government, although this does not appear to have been a concern of early Christians. It is unlikely that any Christians today would defend nondemocratic forms of government, even though these are accepted as the norm in Scripture.[1]

These two distinguishable approaches to ethics sometimes lead to different interpretations of Christian behavior. So, for example, if the Bible regards capital punishment as the appropriate penalty for certain crimes, then presumably there are upholders of the first approach who would say that this penalty still applies, whereas the second approach might argue that this penalty may no longer apply. And there are a couple of cases of scholars adopting the first approach who have been, at the very least, muted in their criticism of slavery.[2]

---

1. To take up the topic of slavery again: presumably, most Christians would consider it right and indeed necessary not only to refrain from practicing it themselves, but also to campaign against it, both in its traditional forms and in situations where people might be regarded as slaves to some other type of bondage, such as tyrannical government or economic oppression.

2. As late as the 1950s and 1960s some respected Christian scholars argued that slavery was still a permissible institution. J. Murray (*Principles of Conduct* [London: Tyndale, 1957], 92–103) holds that Scripture attacks the abuses rather

This bifurcation is also reflected in the different attitudes of Christians on the controversial questions of the role of women in teaching and leadership in the church and also in the household setting. The one side argues that what is stated in certain passages is binding on believers today and insists on the subordination of wives to their husbands and the exclusion of women from some forms of ministry. The other side holds that the passages to which that appeal is made are no longer binding on Christians today in their original form.

How do we decide between these various possibilities of interpretation?

One possibility is simply that the differences are exegetical.[3] Much of the debate over the place of women in ministry is conducted on the level of exegesis. Nevertheless, one might want to ask why two recent commentaries on the Pastoral Epistles, both by writers sharing much the same exegetical environment, would come up with rather different interpretations of 1 Tim. 2.[4] Something more than exegesis is at work.

Proponents of the first approach argue that there are no grounds for supposing that the biblical teaching on these matters is confined to a first-century occasion and cultural setting, and that the same teaching is to be applied today, perhaps with some adaptation to different circumstances. Church structures today are different from those of the first century, and therefore the precise form of exclusion of women from teaching and leadership may be somewhat different, but the principle of

---

than the institution itself. Cf. H. M. Carson, *Colossians and Philemon* (London: Tyndale, 1960), 21–24.

3. The recent work of David Instone-Brewer (*Divorce and Remarriage in the Bible* [Grand Rapids: Eerdmans, 2002]; much more briefly and accessibly, *Divorce and Remarriage in the Church: Biblical Solutions for Pastoral Realities* [Carlisle: Paternoster, 2003]) has shown that the scriptural teaching about divorce, when understood in light of its Jewish background, allows for more possibilities than simply in cases of adultery. Thus, an exegetical base has been provided for what many Christians have increasingly come to recognize as the solution for cases of domestic abuse and the like where all other options have failed.

4. I trust that I may be pardoned for drawing attention in this way to the commentary by W. D. Mounce in the Word Biblical Commentary and the one by myself in the International Critical Commentary; the author of the former did his research on a concept in the Pastoral Epistles in the department in which I was a teacher (although not his immediate supervisor).

exclusion remains in force. Again, the superordinate husband may well have to grant his subordinate wife appropriate autonomy to make her own decisions within a sphere such as her employment, but he will maintain that this autonomy is always subject to his superordinate authority. In both cases the basic principles can and must be maintained. They are transcultural, and although they may be modified in application, they must be applied nonetheless.

Over against these arguments two responses may be made. The first response is that the appropriate application of the principles in the culture of today may largely amount to nonapplication. Although wives are to be subject to their husbands, in practice this is compatible with something approaching equality in the relationship. This proposal is developed as one possibility by W. J. Webb, who dubs it "ultra-soft patriarchialism." The second response is that the underlying principle of patriarchalism is itself culturally relative and that the status of the principle must be investigated in the light of further exploration of the biblical teaching. Webb appears to incline toward accepting a nonpatriarchal view for today.[5] Perhaps less controversially, it seems to me that the rejection of genocide and slavery and the adoption of democracy are decisions that are not based on change of situation and culture; rather, I would affirm that there has been a legitimate and necessary development in the understanding of Christian ethics.

An interesting example that I have not followed up but that might throw light on the problem is the way in which the Dutch Reformed Church in South Africa did a U-turn on apartheid, which that church previously had considered to be supported by scriptural teaching. What were the determining factors in this very significant change of outlook? Was it the case that people went back to Scripture and asked whether their original exegesis was wrong and now replaced it with better exegesis, or was there more to it? What is it that makes people do exegesis differently? My suspicion is that something more than exegesis is involved, and that presuppositions come into play.

5. W. J. Webb, *Slaves, Women, and Homosexuals: Exploring the Hermeneutics of Cultural Analysis* (Downers Grove, Ill.: InterVarsity, 2001), 241–44.

In his important book mentioned above, Webb develops two further points. His first point is, or should be, noncontroversial in principle. He develops a series of tests by which we may know to what degree a statement is expressed in a cultural form from which it can be separated. What was affirmed or required in one culture is not required in a different cultural setting.[6]

Second, and more important for our present concern, Webb traces what he calls a "redemptive movement" or drive in Scripture that leads us on to a fuller redemption than was envisaged in the New Testament. He is able to show how there is a tendency toward a fuller liberation in the ongoing history of redemption, as can be seen in developments from the Old Testament to the New Testament, and he argues that this can and should be carried further in the church. The movement from forbidding eunuchs to approach the temple to fully incorporating them in the people of God is a good example. Here, it seems, there is a consideration that goes beyond the cultural to establish the legitimacy of some movement and advance in ethics.[7]

A further contribution is made by C. H. Cosgrove.[8] In a recent book he develops five rules that we can apply in developing moral principles from Scripture.

1. *The purpose (or justification) behind a biblical moral rule carries greater weight than the rule itself.* By this he means that we need to go behind the rule to see why it is given, and this is more important than the particular formulation, which may be situation-bound, or culturally bound, or limited to one specific application, in which case we need to reformulate the application and even extend it. This is another way of saying that we must get behind the application to the underlying principle, but it substitutes the idea of purpose for principle.

---

6. At least I thought that this was the generally accepted position until I came across an unpublished article in which the writer seemed to be arguing that it was providential that Scripture was given in the conditions of the first century and that God intended us to carry over its cultural practices, specifically in regard to the subordination of women, into our own culture.

7. The idea of a "redemptive trajectory" is not original with Webb. See, for example, R. T. France, *Women in the Church's Ministry: A Test-Case for Biblical Hermeneutics* (Carlisle: Paternoster, 1995).

8. C. H. Cosgrove, *Appealing to Scripture in Moral Debate: Five Hermeneutical Rules* (Grand Rapids: Eerdmans, 2002).

2. *Analogical reasoning is an appropriate and necessary method for applying Scripture to contemporary issues.* This rule scarcely needs justification. It is essentially saying that when we have worked back from biblical moral rules to the underlying principle or purpose, we then must ask what other rules appropriate to our situation can and must be derived from it.

3. *There is a presumption in favor of according greater weight to countercultural tendencies in Scripture that express the voice of the powerless and marginalized than to those tendencies that echo the dominant voices of the culture.* This may be controversial in some quarters, as some people would argue that all scriptural commands stand on the same level. We have learned from the mistakes made by redaction critics not to underestimate the importance of the material taken over by an author from tradition or other sources compared with the author's own contribution to the text. Nevertheless, when Jesus tells people to love their enemies, which does go against the culture, we do pay more attention to what he says. After all, a major element in Christianity is that Jesus taught things that had not been taught previously. We do in fact accept this principle when, for example, we recognize the way in which biblical writers may have tolerated the practice of slavery because it was part of the culture but go on to say things that begin to subvert it.

4. *Scientific (or "empirical") knowledge stands outside the scope of Scripture.* This is to say that where biblical moral rules assume some particular account of reality that we no longer share, the moral rules can no longer apply in their original form. So, for example, if the Old Testament prohibition against eating pork rests to some extent on the way in which food poisoning can easily arise with that particular meat, then the fact that we can render it safe for consumption through refrigeration and other hygienic measures entails that we may be able to dispense with that law. Again, this is controversial for some people.

5. *Moral-theological considerations should guide hermeneutical choices between conflicting plausible interpretations.* Cosgrove applies this by saying that a principle such as the law of love must dominate when conflicting interpretations are on offer. He cites the Scots Confession of 1560, which said, "We dare not receive or admit any interpretation which is contrary to any principal point of our faith, or to any other plain text of Scripture, or to

the rule of love."[9] Interestingly, this citation lists three authorities and not just one, whereas some modern interpreters seem to reduce the list to the one principle of love. Thereby they may fail in practice to recognize that not all love is rightly inspired and conducted, and that true love must be governed by principle. A misuse of the principle of love can lead to a wrong treatment of convicted criminals or to the defense of homosexual practices that go against some fairly plain biblical teaching.

It will be evident that these rules are not free from problems, but they may help to expose some of the problems with which we need to deal, and if we follow the Scots Confession rather than the somewhat truncated fifth principle framed by Cosgrove, we may make some progress.

At this stage, however, I am not trying to provide answers to questions, but simply to illustrate the fact that there are two approaches to questions of ethics. Ethical development does take place within Scripture and the Christian church, although there are differences regarding the ways in which we may or should go beyond Scripture. But the same is true also in the two other spheres of worship and theology.

Two Approaches to Worship

A second area that illustrates essentially the same issues is that of worship. A classical contrast is the one made between the approaches of the Anglicans and the Puritans. The Anglicans adopted the so-called *normative* principle, which "upheld the authority of Scripture inasmuch as no practice directly condemned by the Bible should be countenanced in public worship: 'What the Scripture forbids not, it allows; and what it allows is not unlawful; and what is not unlawful may lawfully be done.'" However, the Puritans followed the so-called *regulative* principle, and in this case the authority of Scripture was upheld "by allowing in public worship only those practices that are either commanded in the New Testament or have biblical warrant in the practice

9. Ibid., 161. The Scots Confession acquired a new lease on life in 1937–38, when Karl Barth delivered his Gifford Lectures based on it at the University of Aberdeen, published as *The Knowledge of God and the Service of God according to the Teaching of the Reformation* (London: Hodder & Stoughton, 1938).

of the New Testament Church. In the words of the Westminster Confession of Faith: 'The acceptable way of worshipping the true God is instituted by himself, and so limited by his own revealed will, that he may not be worshipped according to the imaginations and devices of men, or the suggestions of Satan, under any visible representation, or any other way not prescribed in the holy scriptures.'"[10]

Both approaches taken to extremes could lead to ways of worship that many of us would find unduly restrictive or sadly at odds with the spirit of the New Testament. Obviously, the latter principle is one that prevents any developments in worship that are not sanctioned by Scripture, and this could explain the resistance to instrumental music (especially the "kist o' whistles" [pipe organ], which was frowned upon in some Scottish denominations) and the restriction to psalmody in some Reformed churches. The former might be thought to allow for almost anything that is not forbidden by Scripture, such as elaborate vestments and imposing a fixed lectionary upon leaders of services.

No doubt there has to be some flexibility with either approach. In practice, defenders of the normative principle may feel that it is appropriate on occasion to find scriptural teaching that implicitly forbids some of the things that do not appear to be explicitly banned; equally, defenders of the regulative principle may need to plead for legitimate extensions of biblical practices. The important point for us is that the Puritan approach seems to stifle any development in ways of worship, while the Anglican approach leaves the way open and may be thought to encourage it.

So we see two types of approach: (1) a fairly conservative one that tends to adopt the plain sense of Scripture as it was practiced back then to be binding upon us today unless there are strong reasons for claiming that the circumstances and culture require a modification; (2) a less conservative one that tends to go beyond

10. Extracts from a lecture by Gwyn Davies, "The Puritan Approach to Worship," *Foundations* 48 (spring 2002): 48–49. The quotations are from John Owen (summarizing an Anglican view) and the Westminster Confession of Faith, Chapter XXI.

Scripture by recognizing that some practices are relativized and that in other cases we must extrapolate from Scripture.

But again the key question is how it is that these two approaches arise, and whether there are any principles that might enable us to determine their validity. For in both cases developments do take place. It is hard to believe that any congregational meeting today would fit New Testament practice, even allowing for the inevitable shifts due to changes in cultural setting. So how do we adjudge the legitimacy of changes and developments?

Two Approaches to Doctrine

A third area, more basic than ethics or church order, is theology, and it is this aspect of the biblical material that seems to me to have been given much less attention. All the examples that I have given so far are concerned with the *application* of Scripture to contemporary believers, with questions of behavior. But we are also concerned with what we are to believe and how to express that *belief*.

Perhaps the first thing I need to do is to illustrate the fact that all of us do in fact go beyond Scripture in our doctrine. There is such a thing as development in doctrine.

Two noncontroversial examples prove my point. First, the Formula of Chalcedon is an obvious example of a doctrinal statement that may be implied by Scripture but certainly is not found in so many words in Scripture and probably would have been thought quite strange by first-century Christians; nevertheless, it has become a standard of orthodoxy in regard to the person of Jesus Christ, although it is a standard that is constantly being discussed to ascertain whether it is the most appropriate way to account for the scriptural evidence.

Second, the doctrine of the atonement has found many different forms of expression. Medieval satisfaction theories can be regarded as one attempt to explain its significance in a way that would be intelligible and helpful to Christians at that time. From the Reformation onwards we have the use of the term "penal substitution" to explain the rationale of what goes on in biblical teaching, although neither of the words is strictly biblical. The Christians who propounded these doctrinal formulations saw no incongruity between their acceptance of Scripture as authoritative and their attempts to express its teaching or the implications of its teaching in ways that would take it further than its original expression.

That process continues today, and it raises large questions among evangelical Christians. These questions arise because the process is often controversial. Here I list six examples to illustrate the breadth and importance of the issue.

1. There is what is known as *open theism*, which explores ways of understanding the nature and will of God that differ at significant points from what has been assumed as "classical" theism. Some evangelicals would see this as a legitimate, fresh understanding of biblical teaching, while others would label this outlook heretical.

2. Some recent theologians, attempting to understand the nature of punishment in nonretributive terms, have gone on to question whether *penal substitution* is the basic central core of the Christian understanding of the cross as God's saving action. The question here is not whether penal substitution is taught at all in Scripture (which, in my view, would be hard to deny), but whether it is the primary motif that underlies all the varied imagery used in the Bible and is therefore the key category for systematic theology.

3. Is *infant baptism* a proper development of New Testament doctrine and practice?

4. Are *people who have not heard the gospel* necessarily condemned to hell automatically? Can they plead for mercy on the grounds of ignorance, as 1 Tim. 1:13 might imply?

5. Many evangelical Christians (particularly in the United Kingdom) belong to *episcopal churches* that are not prepared to accept the possibility of full intercommunion with churches that do not have bishops who have been consecrated into what they call the "historic episcopate," whereas other evangelicals believe that the "historic episcopate" is an indefensible concept.[11]

6. For some evangelical Christians the bread and the cup at the *Lord's Supper* are nothing more than physical symbols for the Lord Jesus, with whom the participants have a very real

11. One hopes that, as individuals, these Christians would differ from their denominations in this matter, but nevertheless they are constrained in what they may do by their denominational allegiance.

spiritual fellowship in the meal, whereas for others the bread and the cup are in some sense united with the body and blood of Jesus so that in the physical actions of taking and eating and drinking the participants actually receive Jesus.

These six examples concern issues where there is debate and difference between evangelical Christians as they wrestle with the question of the development and the expression of Christian doctrine. And they are questions of the same kind as those that arise in the realm of Christian practice, since the line between doctrine and practice inevitably is a fuzzy one. Again, it probably is fair to speak of two approaches, conservative and progressive, but it is obvious that the degree of acceptance of these "developments" would be very varied. So my point is confirmed and illustrated: there is development in doctrine, but not all developments appear to be valid. How can we decide which developments are legitimate?

There has been much more methodological discussion of the way in which we interpret the ethics in Scripture than of the way in which we generate doctrine from Scripture. Is it possible to make any progress on these questions? Can we find any principles to guide us? The issues are, of course, related, since very often the ethical commands rest on doctrinal considerations; even so, it is fair to say that most often it is ethics and worship that are regarded as being open to modification in light of situation and culture, whereas it is commonly assumed that doctrine is a matter of unchanging, eternal principles.

Development in Doctrine in the Bible

The common feature in all of my examples is that they are concerned with *development in doctrine*. They are concerned with the making of doctrinal statements that go beyond the express teaching of Scripture. These arise in a number of interrelated ways, of which I will mention four.

First, some questions develop out of *the progress of knowledge or the expansion of the areas in which doctrinal statements are needed.* For example, scientific hypotheses about cosmology and biology raise questions that no one could have envisaged in biblical times about the doctrine of creation, the status of a fetus, and so on.

Second, there is the need *to explain the various statements in Scripture* on a particular topic, and the explanation provided may be one that was not held in that form by any scriptural author. The Formula of Chalcedon says things that New Testament authors could not have said in their own time but is nevertheless meant to offer an understanding of the person of Jesus Christ that will account for the various ways in which he is described in the New Testament. "Penal substitution" is not a biblical expression; it had not occurred to the New Testament writers, but it could be the underlying principle that explains what is actually said about the significance of the death of Jesus.

Third, problems arise because *different texts stand in tension* with one another, and some way of harmonizing and synthesizing them is sought, although the individual authors probably were not aware of the tensions between, say, texts that imply the conscious eternal suffering of the wicked and those that imply some other fate. Or there are the two ways in which Scripture speaks of God in relation to people, whether as a partner in dialogue or as the potter who makes the pots exactly the way that he wants them to be.

Fourth, still other questions may arise out of tensions that are felt between biblical teachings and what I will call the *insights of minds nurtured on the gospel*. It can be argued that a biblically based, Christian understanding of love and justice that forbids us to practice torture conflicts with the belief that God can consign unrepentant sinners to an eternal punishment that appears to consist of conscious torment expressed in the imagery of eternal fire. Cases like this are similar to my third category, but here I am looking more at conflict between specific teachings and general principles than between conflicting specific teachings.

My basic motivation in this series of lectures is that *it is especially the duty of evangelical Christians to provide some kind of reasoned, principled approach to the question of the development of doctrine from Scripture.* If we of all Christians claim to believe in the continuing authority of Scripture and its relevance to our contemporary world, then it is all the more incumbent upon us to provide a reasoned statement of the path from the Bible to the modern world and vice versa. This challenge has been taken up in various contemporary projects that aim at bridging the gap between the Bible and the church or between the Bible and systematic theology.[12] Nevertheless, I have looked in vain for helpful discussion of precisely this point: is there a principled way of moving from the Bible to doctrine?

One or two introductory points are needed in order to clarify what I am trying to do.

Who Calls the Shots?

Let me return to a point that I adumbrated at the end of the first lecture. Right at the outset of our exploration it is essential to distinguish what I am trying to do from what may be called a *liberal* approach. Liberalism interprets Scripture and formulates doctrine by the measure of what contemporary people can believe and practice. The result has been that it is our surrounding culture and worldview that dictate what can be accepted from Scripture and what should be rejected as unacceptable to "modern" people and, as we must now presumably go on to say, "postmodern" people. Such trimming of the faith subjects the teaching of the Bible to the changing, arbitrary shifts of contemporary opinion and rests on no firm principles. So we have seen, for example, the rejection of the miraculous and the dislike of sacrificial understandings of the death of Christ accompanied by some kind of "reinterpretation" of Scripture. Possibly, "reinterpretation" is the wrong word here; for some liberals it is more a matter of rejection than reinterpretation.

Some evangelicals tend to dismiss the liberal approach out of hand, but we cannot simply write off the concerns felt by liberals. We must carefully distinguish between the liberal dismissal of parts of Scripture and the motivation that leads to it. A more sound approach would include the recognition that the liberal Christian mind, and to some extent the contemporary secular mind, may also be shaped by principles that ultimately are inspired by the Christian message or are in harmony with

12. Examples are the Scripture and Hermeneutics Seminar; the "Between Two Horizons" commentary series, edited by J. B. Green and M. Turner; and the work of F. B. Watson.

it.[13] Thus, if minds nurtured at least to some extent by the gospel come to conclusions that seem to clash with what is taken to be scriptural teaching, then this establishes a prima facie case for reconsideration of whether we have correctly identified the latter. I emphasize that reconsideration is not the same thing as rejection or rewriting. What we are seeing is nothing more than an amber light that signifies that something needs examination. In many cases, the problem may lie rather with the contemporary mind that needs to be corrected by Scripture. The wholesale rejection of the supernatural is the obvious example. In other cases, instead of the modern culture and worldview dictating the jettisoning of something in Scripture, the existence of a clash serves as an indicator that there is a problem that needs a solution. Thus, on the one side, the so-called scientific worldview that denies the possibility of miracles cannot be allowed to call the shots, and a Christian worldview based on Scripture will rightly recognize that here it is the modern worldview that is defective and needs to be revised. On the other side, the availability of appropriate medical facilities means that mothers now have aids to alleviate the pain of childbirth, and presumably no one would argue that it is wrong to use such aids because the existence of the curse in Gen. 3:16 implicitly forbids attempts to escape from its consequences. But how do we know which is the right possibility in any given case?

The Challenge of Scripture Itself

A second element is the recognition that Scripture can continue to speak in fresh ways to its readers. This is expressed well by R. B. Hays, who labels "the quest for hermeneutical closure" an illusion. "Texts will always demand and generate new interpretation," Hays contends.[14] This is a modern way of expressing the classic principle of Puritan John Robinson: "The Lord hath yet more truth and light to break forth from his

13. For example, the recognition of human beings as persons of inherent worth and dignity and not as mere things or disposable objects may rest ultimately upon the biblical doctrine of creation in the image of God or at least be in harmony with it.

14. R. B. Hays, *Echoes of Scripture in the Letters of Paul* (New Haven: Yale University Press, 1989), 4.

holy Word." To some of us this may be a disturbing principle. It implies that we can never come to the end of being surprised by Scripture, although we probably would prefer to have a secure belief system whereby we are no longer challenged by God in new ways.

But, granted that fresh significance emerges in the encounter between the Word and its readers, how can we know what counts as *truth and light?* Can we advance any principled criteria for the development and evaluation of fresh insights?

Scriptural Principles for Going beyond Scripture?

My intuition is that if we are directed by Scripture as our authority in *what* we are to believe and do, then we are also directed in our investigation of *how* we are to interpret Scripture by Scripture itself rather than by any overriding external authority. What we need, then, is some kind of *scriptural* approach to the problem of development and interpretation. Can we establish principles that are rooted in the statements and the practice of Scripture that will enable us to make progress in framing interpretative procedures and guard us against invalid interpretations and false conclusions? We thus have to look for some principled way of dealing with such matters, and it is here that the debate will center for some time to come.

Our agenda is now set. We are to look for possible clues to an answer to our problem by looking into the Bible itself to see how Christian teaching developed and whether any principles can be found that controlled the development. Such principles may be implicit rather than explicit.

The Fact and Nature of Development within Scripture

In order to establish a basis for the proposals that I will offer in the next lecture, we will make a quick survey of some of the things that can be seen happening in the New Testament. Early Christians had various sources for their teaching, and they did some interesting things with them. What we repeatedly observe is that in various ways they built on their sources but went beyond them. We see this happening in three areas of development. The result of such development is, inevitably, diversity, both between earlier and later material, but also between different developments that stand alongside one another.

The Use of the Old Testament

The first Christians recognized the Jewish Scriptures as their own Scriptures. The influence of Scripture on their thinking was wide and profound, even where scriptural citations and allusions are not present. Scripture provided the framework within which they thought by offering a worldview and a "Godview" that they took over without question. To be sure, what they took over was refracted to some extent by the Judaism within which they were nurtured, but basically they understood themselves to be controlled by Scripture.

Yet they clearly went beyond that worldview in certain ways. Here I will offer five examples.

1. The Old Testament already had an understanding of *God as Father*. Early Christians developed it in two ways. First, although this description is comparatively rare in the Old Testament, it became the central category for the understanding of the nature of God and his relationship to his people. Second, whereas in the Old Testament this description seems to have been essentially an analogical one according to which God treats his people like a parent treats children and expects appropriate behavior in return, in the New Testament the understanding seems to become more personal and ontological. Although in some places the relation of believers to God is expressed in terms of adoption, there is also the clear teaching on new birth or regeneration by the Holy Spirit, which suggests something much more in terms of being than simply relationship.

2. The understanding of God himself was taken further in that it became possible to think of God as being identifiable not only as God the Father, but also explicitly as God the Son and less explicitly as God the Spirit. The concept of a *threefoldness* in God is simply not present in the Old Testament, although Christians would have insisted that it was consistent with the

Old Testament, since they were not thinking of three Gods, but of one God in three persons.[15]

3. The concept of *the people of God* in the Old Testament is very much cast in terms of Israel as his special people, although this does not exclude the nations from God's concern. However, the idea of non-Jews becoming part of this special people, and especially of them being the majority group within it, is for the most part a fringe matter.

4. The concept of an *afterlife* in which the righteous are with God and the unrighteous are judged is, again, on the fringe and plays no vital part in much of Old Testament religion, whereas for Christians it is central.

5. In its canonical form the *legislation* in the Pentateuch determines the life of the people of God, but for New Testament Christians this is no longer the case, at least so far as what can be regarded as specifically Jewish legislation is concerned (often understood as "ritual," but again the border is fuzzy).

These five examples illustrate how various characteristic New Testament developments are from motifs that were already present to some extent on the fringe of the Old Testament; however, we must recognize that moving them to center stage leads to decisive changes in their content and their significance. This is analogous to how, for example, the nature of a friendship with a woman on the fringe of a man's life changes character enormously if she moves to the center of it.

For the moment, we are simply observing that development has taken place along these lines. Nevertheless, we must try later to understand the nature of these developments.

The Teaching of Jesus

A second element influencing the early Christians was the teaching of Jesus. Manifestly this was the major factor in taking Christians beyond the teaching of the Old Testament. Yet here

---

15. Some Christian interpreters would claim that the Old Testament can be read in a "trinitarian" way—for example, when Christ is identified with some Old Testament figure(s)—but certainly this was not how the original authors understood what they wrote.

again there was development beyond the teaching of Jesus. Two processes are in action here.

First, the teaching of the early Christians was not limited to the repetition of what Jesus taught, but involved *the proclamation of him* as the crucified, risen, and returning Savior and Lord who is spiritually related to his people here and now. Even where the teaching of Jesus influences the letter writers, there is scarcely any direct citation of what he said, but rather allusion and echo. And this is the case even on the most maximalist estimates of its impact.[16] This is a shift in emphasis of enormous significance.

Second, even where Jesus' teaching is recounted, it is possible for it to be given in *a new form* that, while clearly in continuity with it, differs remarkably in expression and in the resultant impact. We are unlikely to get a better informed, more well-grounded presentation of the historical reliability of the Gospel of John than that of C. L. Blomberg, but he recognizes throughout that there has been some transmutation of the teaching using different modes of expression, and I see that recognition as unavoidable. Blomberg explicitly says, "The freedom [John] felt to select, interpret, abridge and elaborate on the works and words of the historical Jesus doubtless stemmed from his sense of the Spirit's inspiration depicted here." And again he writes of John's "freedom to write up his material as distinctively as he did" while limiting "himself to what Jesus really did and taught."[17]

This phenomenon is not confined to John's Gospel. The fact that we have four canonical Gospels, and that there may have been other quasi-evangelical documents (such as Q or the "attempts" referred to by Luke in the prologue of his Gospel) shows that different Christians saw the need for fresh retellings of the story of Jesus that were shaped by the particular situations in which they found themselves. Even on the most conservative of hypotheses, it is evident that the evangelists worked creatively, either on a common pool of tradition or on a mixture of sources both oral and written, in such ways that they made different selections of material to include and edited what they

16. D. Wenham, *Paul: Follower of Jesus or Founder of Christianity?* (Grand Rapids: Eerdmans, 1995).

17. C. L. Blomberg, *The Historical Reliability of John's Gospel* (Leicester: Apollos, 2001), 203, 292.

did include in different ways.[18] The result is that we have four readily distinguishable portraits of Jesus that can be regarded as developments of whatever lay behind them. This is not to say that the developments are incompatible with one another, but that they are written from different perspectives.[19]

As a result of these two processes we can see various specific developments taking place.

The central theme in the teaching of Jesus was the kingdom of God, but this motif moves away from the center in the teaching of the early Christians. It is not that it is denied, but rather that it is found to be less and less appropriate for expressing the heart of the matter. The center lies rather in the personal relationship of believers to the risen and exalted Lord, a relationship made possible by his atoning death.

Consequently, although the teaching of Jesus did lie at the base of apostolic teaching, it was possible for early Christians to reinterpret it or go beyond it in some ways. There can be a shift in idiom. Teaching about following Jesus as disciples is found in the Synoptic Gospels, but in Paul's writings this is no longer appropriate, and teaching about the imitation of Christ may be regarded as the equivalent to it. Christians were particularly conscious of the continuing presence of Jesus, with whom they had some kind of contact that is expressed in various metaphors, sometimes those of ordinary human relationships (knowing Christ; trusting in Christ; feelings of loving and being loved), but also the language of Christ being in them or of their being in Christ or of mutual indwelling; God the Father and the Holy Spirit are referred to in similar ways.

Developments within Apostolic Teaching

The early church also developed its theology in various ways. I will draw my examples from the Pastoral Epistles, although these three phenomena can be traced in the earlier letters of Paul.

18. This is an attempt to make my point regardless of whether one accepts different sources or a common tradition that can be reconstructed by harmonizing the account.

19. See S. C. Barton, "Many Gospels, One Jesus?" in *The Cambridge Companion to Jesus* (ed. M. Bockmuehl; Cambridge: Cambridge University Press, 2001), 170–83.

First, there is *the apostolic deposit*. The Pauline writings attach considerable importance to the preservation of tradition handed down in the church and considered to be authoritative. There is a basic body of sound teaching that is to be preserved unchanged and handed down to those who will continue to teach in the church (2 Tim. 1:13–14; 2:2). Nevertheless, the teaching of Paul (or whoever wrote the Pastoral Epistles) goes beyond the "deposit" and expresses the faith in new ways.

Second, there are *further revelations*. In one place we are told what "the Spirit clearly says" about what will happen in the last days (1 Tim. 4:1), presumably through a prophetic saying (cf. 1 Tim. 1:18; 4:14). There is reference to a "mystery," which generally refers to something previously hidden but now revealed by God (1 Tim. 3:16). New teaching thus is given, and this itself may lead to further developments. We see this particularly in the communication of mysteries in the earlier Pauline writings.

Third, there is *reaction to erroneous teaching*. Teaching that was not in accord with Pauline teaching was an ongoing problem. Although time was not to be wasted in responding to empty speculations, there are places where a response to false teaching leads to fresh formulations (1 Tim. 4:1–5; 6:6–10); earlier, the teaching of Judaizers was responsible for inciting Paul to major developments in the doctrine of justification.

These three factors combined to produce a reaffirmation of existing Christian teaching coupled with developments of it in light of further insight and as a reaction to the false teaching. The central core of doctrinal teaching—"the tradition" or "the gospel" or "the word"—is applied in various ways to contingent situations and is itself modified and developed in the process of application. Although it has been argued that Timothy was supposed to reproduce the earlier teaching in an unchanged form, a more or less word-for-word reproduction of what he was taught, it is clear that there was change and development. This is shown by the way in which the author of the letters uses a vocabulary different from that found in the earlier letters of Paul and through it expresses Christian truth in fresh ways, with different emphases and nuances. Whether the author was Paul or a disciple is immaterial to the issue. Whoever wrote the letters did not feel tied to the manner of expression of the earlier Paul.

The Closing of the Canon: Going beyond the Canon

At the end of this process we have the production of the New Testament writings. They bear silent testimony to a series of developments in which there is continuity with what has gone before, but also there are shifting emphases with corresponding shifts in character. Thus, they exhibit a certain untidiness in which not everything is cut and dried. Development therefore can lead to a diversity that may be not much more than a difference in expression or a clearer enunciation of latent theological ideas, but may also create a certain amount of tension.

The question that arises is whether such productions, recognized by later Christians as "canon," constitute a conclusion to doctrinal and ethical development or whether they offer a pattern that the church can continue to follow.

Here, an important distinction must be made between the production of further Scriptures, which is ruled out by the creation of the canon as a closed list, and the development of doctrine and practice on the basis of those canonical writings. *The closing of the canon is not incompatible with the nonclosing of the interpretation of that canon.* The church, under divine guidance, has established the canon, and I will assume that it cannot be changed. The church believes that its faith and practice rest upon that collection of books and that no others can have that function. Yet the closing of the canon did not bring the process of doctrinal development to an end. Thus, the question of the interpretation of Scripture remains open. So what remains to be done is to take a further look at some aspects of the process that we have been describing to see if any guidelines emerge for the church's continuing task of theological development.

3

The Search
for Biblical Principles

In the previous chapter I attempted to do three things. First, I
tried to show that currently there are two approaches to Scripture, or at least two tendencies, one of which asserts that what
Scripture teaches remains essentially in force today although
some teaching may have been given in a situation-specific and
culture-specific form, whereas the other allows that there can
be and is development beyond scriptural teaching in theology,
ecclesiology, and ethics. Second, I illustrated the fact that developments have taken place in doctrinal teaching, whether legitimately or otherwise, and argued that we need some criteria
for assessing the validity of these developments. Third, I showed
that development in doctrine is nothing new, but was already
going on in Scripture itself. But how, if at all, can we go on developing doctrine beyond what we find has already happened in
Scripture? Our agenda now is to ask whether the development
of doctrine within Scripture legitimates continuing development
and provides criteria for how we should go about it.

Interpretation of the Old Testament

First, let us consider what was actually happening when the New Testament writers made use of the Old Testament. On the basis of the use of the Old Testament in the New Testament I wish to suggest that texts that had a particular authoritative meaning in their original setting may have a different authoritative meaning in a different setting. There is room for looking at only one specific, limited example out of the five that I gave in the previous lecture, namely, the doctrine that underlies Old Testament legislation, and I will narrow this down even further to a consideration of *Leviticus*. Although Leviticus is very much a book about laws and commands, the underlying doctrine is of basic importance. Here is a quick survey of the main references to it in the New Testament:

1. The requirement concerning sacrifice in Lev. 12:8 is carried out by the parents of Jesus, who are still living under the old covenant even after his birth (Luke 2:24).

2. The teaching about keeping oaths in Lev. 19:12 is cited by Jesus in Matt. 5:33, and it is in a sense left standing but superseded by a higher principle of not making oaths at all. Either Jesus is saying, "This Scripture is rendered obsolete for my disciples because they should not make oaths at all," or he perhaps is saying, "If you do make an oath, keep it; but really you should not need to make oaths at all." In any case, whereas Leviticus assumes that people do make oaths, Jesus goes beyond it by saying that his followers should not do so, and that was not said in Leviticus.

3. The commandment to love one's neighbor in Lev. 19:18 is cited several times with approval as part of a summation of the law. In Matt. 5:43 it implicitly remains in force, because if you are to love your enemies, then a fortiori you are to love your neighbors. Matthew 19:19 adds this commandment to the requirements imposed on the rich young man by Jesus. Matthew 22:39 states the two commandments that are "greatest" in the law. In Rom. 13:9 and Gal. 5:14 Paul sees this commandment as equivalent to or summing up all other commandments (including the second part of the Decalogue), so that by loving other people, one fulfills the law. James 2:8 commends obedience to it as the "royal law," that is, the law of the King or of the kingdom.

4. First Peter 1:16 cites Lev. 19:2, "You shall be holy," with approval and applies it to the new people of God generally.[1] Paul cites Lev. 26:12 in 2 Cor. 6:16 to justify his belief that believers constitute a temple in which God is present with them, and therefore they are to be holy and free from evil.

5. The statement in Lev. 18:5 that "the person who does them [statutes and ordinances] shall live by them" is countered by Paul in Rom. 10:5 with a statement about righteousness by faith with the implication that the principle no longer stands; similarly in Gal. 3:12.

6. Hebrews contains an account of the Jewish sacrificial system largely based on Leviticus, but sees it as a foreshadowing of the sacrifice of Christ and now no longer required.[2]

7. Although there is no express citation, the reference to impure and unclean animals whose flesh Peter is unwilling to eat in Acts 10:9–16 rests upon Lev. 11, where there is a clear prohibition against eating them. In the vision Peter hears a voice saying that he is not to consider what God has cleansed to be impure (v. 15). In the context Peter takes this as permission to go to a Gentile house, and he no longer regards Gentiles as unclean. It seems most likely that the heavenly voice was declaring both foods and people to be clean, since the accusation later brought against Peter is not that he evangelized Gentiles, but that he ate with them (Acts 11:3); thus, a divine fiat indicates that a regulation under the old covenant no longer applies.[3]

8. In Acts 15:20, 28–29 the so-called apostolic decree in effect requires converted Gentiles to refrain from food sacrificed to idols, blood, the meat of strangled animals, and sexual immorality. One interpretation of this passage is that it refers to the

1. The case for a wider dependence on Lev. 19 in 1 Pet. 1:13–2:10 is made by W. L. Schutter, *Hermeneutic and Composition in I Peter* (Wissenschaftliche Untersuchungen zum Neuen Testament 2.30; Tübingen: Mohr, 1989). The summons to holiness from Leviticus dominates this section, although Schutter's individual detailed suggestions are less convincing.

2. In Acts 3:23 Peter cites the wording of Lev. 23:29 to indicate the fate of people disobedient to the coming prophet (although it originally applies to people who do not observe the Day of Atonement).

3. The interpretation of the incident is disputed, and some take it that the vision is to be applied only on the allegorical level to people and not to foods. For this view, see C. A. Miller, "Did Peter's Vision in Acts 10 Pertain to Men or the Menu?" *Bibliotheca Sacra* 159 (2002): 302–17.

rules in Lev. 17–18 that applied to Jews and resident aliens in the land. It then can be argued that the provisions in Leviticus for resident aliens were regarded as still applying to Gentiles who were now part of the people of God in the church. They were not required to become Jewish proselytes and keep all of the law, but only those parts of it that were required of Gentiles resident in the land. The assumption then must be that Jewish converts were still keeping the law of Moses.[4] This interpretation leaves some matters up in the air. Thus, it does not make clear whether or not Jewish converts would eat foods formerly considered unclean in Christian Gentile homes. And although the decree certainly was followed in some circles for some time, it is not clear whether it was followed universally; M. Bockmuehl argues that it was applicable only within a limited area. In any case, it is likely that Jewish Christians continued to maintain their customs and did not suddenly and swiftly adopt a Gentile way of life. It may be, therefore, that in light of Acts 15 we should not interpret Acts 10–11 to apply to a change of menu. For the moment I leave this issue open.

This short list enables us to see the following points:

1. Life under the old covenant involving the offering of sacrifice continues up to and including the time of Jesus, who naturally assumes this in his teaching (Matt. 5:23–24). However, after his death the sacrificial legislation is treated as obsolete, although it served as a foreshadowing of the sacrifice of Christ.

2. Teaching is given by Jesus that goes beyond the law and presumably still applies to believers.

3. The assumption is that the law (as now amended) is to be fulfilled by followers of Jesus and all subsequent believers (both Jewish and Gentile), and the law is seen as being summed up in the command to love one's neighbor.

4. Nevertheless, the statement that people will live—that is, be justified—by observing the law is set aside explicitly by Paul. Paul, then, no longer sees obedience to the law as the way of

---

4. So R. Bauckham, "James and the Gentiles (Acts 15.13–21)," in *History, Literature and Society in the Book of Acts* (ed. B. Witherington III; Cambridge: Cambridge University Press, 1996), 154–84, esp. 172–79. Cf. M. Bockmuehl, *Jewish Law in Gentile Churches: Halakhah and the Beginning of Christian Public Ethics* (Edinburgh: Clark, 2000), 49–83, 145–73.

justification, but nevertheless the law can prescribe how to live (note Rom. 13 and the stress on holiness in Matthew).

If we try to discover what principles control this interpretation, the following seem to apply:

1. There is an old/new covenant distinction (most fully expressed in Hebrews). This way of putting the matter implies both continuity, in that both are covenants, and discontinuity, in that one is old and the other is new. The problem is to discern in what ways the new differs from the old.

2. The material sacrifices, usually of animals, are understood as temporary pointers to the death of Jesus. They provide categories for understanding it, but in so doing they render themselves obsolete. The writer to the Hebrews knows that they are provided as the pattern for understanding Jesus and recognizes that physical blood cannot atone for sins. Thus, there is a new significance given to the texts in Leviticus that was not apparent to the original readers but is now apparent to Christian believers. These texts now are read not as instructions to be carried out, but as teaching that provides categories for understanding the significance of the death of Jesus. Thus, they are read in a different way from that which presumably was in the mind of the human author and the original readers, even though we may want to say that God as the ultimate author foresaw and intended the rereading.

3. There is scholarly uncertainty as to whether the clean/unclean foods distinction no longer applies. It seems clear that it was not required of Gentile believers, since it is not present in the apostolic decree or anywhere else. The question is whether it was still required of Jewish believers. It can be assumed that many of them, if not all, continued to maintain it out of long-standing custom. They are not told that they must abandon the practice. Nevertheless, there is some debate here. Messianic Jews agree with many scholars who hold that in the New Testament the Old Testament law is still binding upon Jewish Christians.[5] The interpretation of the teaching of Jesus (Mark 7:19) and of the vision granted to Peter (Acts 10:9–16) is debated, although I side with those who think that the clean/unclean foods distinction is here set aside by God himself. In my view, Rom. 14:14 indicates

5. Most recently, David J. Rudolph, "Jesus and the Food Laws: A Reassessment of Mark 7:19b," *Evangelical Quarterly* 74 (2002): 291–311.

quite clearly that Paul, a Jewish Christian, regarded all foods as clean, but he respected the conscientious views of those who differed with him; the existence of Mark 7:19 indicates that there was uncertainty on the matter that Mark attempted to remove by indicating how the saying of Jesus should be interpreted.

Can we presume that on the basis of this specific point a more general application of the ritual/moral distinction was made? Or was a distinction made between laws (principally ritual) that applied to Jews and those (principally moral) that also applied to Gentiles? Bockmuehl holds that a moral/ritual distinction is unknown, "legally unworkable and practically awkward."[6] I am not so sure.

4. At the same time, it is possible for New Testament authors to cite ethical principles from Leviticus (and elsewhere in the Pentateuch) as still binding upon Christians, to press for believers to be holy, and to require love of their neighbors. But holiness now appears to be a moral and spiritual quality rather than a ritual one.

5. With the exception of whatever ritual or specifically Jewish laws may remain in force, the Scriptures so understood now apply to all of the new covenant people, Jews and Gentiles.

Evidently, the authority of the Pentateuch continues, but it is read in a manner different from what it used to be. The authoritative elements have somehow changed. To express the matter simply in terms of fulfillment taking place in "Christ" is too simple. There is a complex of associated principles that needs to be unpacked. There is a new covenant that applies equally to Jews and to Gentiles, as a consequence of which the sacrifice of Christ replaces the Levitical sacrifices and the ritual laws no longer apply in full or no longer apply at all, but the basic understanding of the need for atonement for sin and of a holy life (now defined exclusively spiritually and ethically) continues. So it may be best to say that it is reading the Old Testament in light of Christ as the inaugurator of the new covenant that is the guiding principle in the present instance.[7] Perhaps there is

---

6. Bockmuehl, *Jewish Law,* 149 n. 14.

7. This reading would claim to be based on the Old Testament as correctly understood, as may be seen from the way in which Paul appeals precisely to the Old Testament itself to justify his own reading of it.

a principle for development in Deut. 18:15 in which Moses is succeeded by other prophets and Christ in particular, whose instructions the people are to obey. This leaves open the possibility of new revelations through the prophet.

In this particular example I contend that there is a principled approach to the Old Testament rather than an ad hoc, arbitrary understanding of it. This may be true elsewhere, but my sample may be too limited to permit wide-ranging conclusions.[8] But I maintain that this principled approach can be seen even if it was not carried out with complete consistency and other phenomena also are present.[9]

The question that now arises is whether the old/new covenant distinction can be extended in application.[10]

In some respects we are witnessing an unstable situation in which development may still go on. Although it is true that Gentile Christians went on observing the apostolic decree in various places for some time,[11] it did not last. Gentile Christians no longer abstain from meat that may have blood in it, with the Scottish "black pudding" being a conspicuous example of this. If the proposals in Acts 15 were intended simply to provide a modus vivendi for Gentiles living with law-keeping Jewish Christians (as Acts 15:21 might be taken to suggest), they are not necessary if the situation changes. Abstinence from idolatrous foods and sexual immorality remain as requirements strongly endorsed by Paul, but the prohibition of blood and nonkosher meat is no longer required. So the question arises of whether we are to see a theology in process of transition. The fact that many millions of Gentile Christians of many denominations do

8. For a different understanding, see A. T. Lincoln, "Abraham Goes to Rome: Paul's Treatment of Abraham in Romans 4," in *Worship, Theology and Ministry in the Early Church: Essays in Honor of Ralph P. Martin* (ed. M. J. Wilkins and T. Paige; Journal for the Study of the New Testament: Supplement Series 87; Sheffield: JSOT Press, 1992), 163–79.

9. Our concern here is with the Old Testament as a source of teaching. The interpretation of predictive prophecy and related matters, such as the use of typology, raise other questions.

10. J. D. G. Dunn (*The Living Word* [London: SCM, 1987], 126–36) offers a discussion, along lines similar to mine, on relativity between the old and the new covenants, but he observes that it cannot be extended to material in the New Testament itself.

11. Bockmuehl, *Jewish Law,* 166–67.

not confine themselves to kosher meat shows that the church has not regarded the decree as an unchangeable law.[12]

I suggest that the theological basis for the obsolete parts of the decree has ceased to exist. The prohibition against blood in Leviticus is related to the use of the physical blood of animals for making atonement; once this practice ceased because of the death of Jesus, the grounds for the prohibition no longer existed. It is significant that in the verbal allusions to the apostolic decree in Rev. 2:14, 20, only the prohibitions against idolatrous foods and immorality have survived. It may be, therefore, that the apostolic decree is to be seen as no more than a temporary measure for the time being.

There is a parallel in the question of "the land." Although physical geography plays an important role in the Old Testament, I would argue that it has been fully spiritualized in the New Testament, and the land plays no part in Christian theology. This could well be part of a recognition that the writing of the law on the heart leads into a growing spiritualization of religion. For the most part this new attitude is introduced silently in the New Testament, although John 4 is clear testimony to it.

These examples perhaps suggest that to some extent the New Testament situation is one of gradual change from the old covenant situation, a kind of "living between the times," and consequently that further developments may be justified.

Spiritualization under the new covenant must not, of course, be misunderstood. The prohibitions of idolatrous foods and immorality are concerned with actual behavior on a physical level. There are other forms of idolatry besides eating food sacrificed to idols. I believe that at the present time we are in grave danger of idolizing food and especially drink, to say nothing of possessions in general, and that Christians need to take very seriously the prohibition against making idols of material things and physical enjoyment. And although the land, in the sense that I have defined it, no longer plays a role in theology, it is clear that the possession and use of land, as, for example, currently in Zimbabwe, is very much a matter of concern for Christian theology.

12. The fact that in practice it would be impossible to revert to this decree is, of course, not necessarily a justification for not doing so.

We need a Christian theology of land that gets us beyond what is sometimes a religiously justified nationalism.

The significance of the old/new covenant distinction as an interpretative tool is that it combines the two elements of continuity in that the new is a renewal of the old, and therefore the old is taken up into the new, and that the new is new, and therefore in some ways it supersedes the old.

From Jesus to the Early Church

Let us now look at the shifts from the teaching of Jesus to that of the early church. We have established the fact of this development earlier. Now we are trying to understand what is going on in the process.

So far as the Synoptic Gospels are concerned, they present the teaching of Jesus in the simple terms in which it was given for the benefit of people who had the utmost difficulty in understanding it (even his disciples!) and who were living in the context of Jewish religion and in the period of the dawn of the kingdom of God. Thus, we may say that the teaching of Jesus is constrained by four parameters:

1. It is given in the time of the dawn of the kingdom of God, the period prior to the death and resurrection of Jesus, which dramatically alter the situation.
2. It is elementary instruction because it is for beginners starting from scratch.
3. It is given within the conditions of life under Judaism because it is for the most part addressed to Jews.
4. It uses the imagery and thought forms current at the time.

In order to understand this situation, we may helpfully invoke the concept of the *liminal period,* the stage during which something is coming to birth and therefore is neither completely out of the womb nor completely into independent existence; that is, it is not completely one thing or the other, but belongs to a time of transition. Let us look at each of these four parameters more closely.

1. This means that teaching given in the circumstances of the old covenant, since Jesus could be said to "live between the times," now has to be translated for the new situation, in which Jesus is no longer physically present and in which the new age has fully dawned (even though it is not yet fully consummated).[13] It also means that much new teaching has to be given about the new age itself. So our old/new covenant distinction applies here; that is, the old/new covenant distinction is an interpretative tool that can be used with regard to teaching not only in the Old Testament, but also in the Gospels.

2. For such reasons the teaching of Jesus is to be seen as undeveloped, although it is in line with the later developments of Christology, soteriology, and pneumatology. We have a process at work in which the comparatively elementary teaching of Jesus is taken up by his followers into a fuller understanding that can include it but goes beyond it. This, of course, is by no means to overlook the fact that within these parameters the teaching of Jesus is new and startling in his message of the fulfillment of the prophecy of the coming of the kingdom and in his ethic of love.

This undeveloped character of the teaching can be seen in some examples.

The *Christology* is "elementary": it may have been sufficient for Jesus to get across the concept of the Messiah, which he was filling with new content, but the full implications of sonship and lordship are somewhat on the fringe, although not absent. The result is that a Christology (if we may so call it) of Jesus as prophet and Davidic Messiah is taken up into a deeper understanding of him as Son of God and Lord that is no more than adumbrated in the teaching of Jesus.[14] It is not that the Christology is wrong, but that it is incomplete and undeveloped in such a way that people who held to it later, after development had taken place, could be regarded as heretical (Ebionites). So

13. This may be the element of truth to be retained from H. Conzelmann's idea of "the middle of time"; there is a liminal period between the era of promise and the era of fulfillment because the salvation event is not a matter of a moment of time, but rather is a process.

14. This is not to deny that Jesus' self-understanding went beyond what he felt able to express in his teaching, but it does not affect my basic point concerning what the Gospels actually say.

when we interpret the Christology in the Gospels, we need to do so in the context of the fuller revelation after Easter and to recognize its elementary character.

Similarly, it has been famously said that Jesus could not very well explain the significance of his *death* to people who could not believe that he was going to be put to death. The death of Jesus, seen as something divinely necessitated and as a ransom and sacrifice for many, is taken up into a deeper understanding that begins to be expressed in the eucharistic sayings. I think that a reasonable case can be made that the teaching in Mark 10:45 and 14:22–25 is best understood as the primitive statements out of which the later understanding of redemption developed.[15] But there is more to be said than is said in these two texts.

Similarly, it was nearly impossible to explain the phenomenon of the *Holy Spirit* to disciples so long as Jesus was present with them. Indeed, there is a problem here in that the concept of divine empowering to live as disciples is virtually absent from the teaching of Jesus; it would be going too far to say that the teaching about the help of the Spirit in times of persecution implies that the Spirit's help is given only in special circumstances, but certainly nothing is said to encourage a belief in the continuous working of the Spirit. One can argue that people can become disciples only if there is a prior call by Jesus, but this is not always the case. Reading the Gospels on their own, however, we might conclude that Jesus calls people to be totally committed and to persevere but leaves them to do so in their own strength apart from some limited help from the Spirit. After Easter the provision of the Spirit becomes an almost unexpected reality.

Of particular importance here is the distinction between the time of Jesus' earthly presence with his disciples and his physical absence after the resurrection. This is a major shift that entails the reformulation and development of the teaching of Jesus. This can be seen in the concept of *discipleship*. It is well known that the term "disciple" is not used for believers after Easter except significantly in the writings of Luke, who uses it only in narrative (with the single exception of Acts 15:10) in a way that brings out the identity between the followers of Jesus before Easter and

15. See I. H. Marshall, *Jesus the Saviour: Studies in New Testament Theology* (London: SPCK, 1990), 239–57.

the group of believers after Easter; Luke uses the term of those who become disciples after Easter (as well as those who were already disciples before Easter), but no other New Testament writer does so. There is a development in the concept of what it means to have an attachment to Jesus after Easter, but not of such a nature that the teaching of Jesus cannot be applied to it. Indeed, the Gospels contain statements that are effectively prophetic, such as Matt. 18:20, where everything suggests that this applies to the post-Easter period. Here we have on a small scale what is developed much more in John.

3. The teaching of Jesus may be thought to imply the continuation of Jewish practices by his disciples. Thus, Matt. 6 may be thought to require disciples to continue the Jewish practice of fasting, although it may be that what Jesus is really talking about is an attitude exemplified in fasting rather than commending the practice itself. As already noted, he also teaches about what to do when one is making an offering in the temple, although this practice soon became obsolete for his disciples. But he could hardly teach otherwise than by reference to attitudes to be adopted within the practices of the time.

4. The imagery used by Jesus is sometimes what his audience would understand, but this accommodation may lead to misunderstanding. In a number of parables spoken by Jesus the protagonist condemns unworthy servants to horrendous fates. The imprisonment and torture of the unforgiving servant is followed by the warning that such punishment is how "my heavenly Father will treat each of you" (Matt. 18:35). The wicked servant is cut in pieces and assigned a place with the unbelievers (Matt. 24:51//Luke 12:46). The people who failed to help Christ by failing to help those in need are assigned to eternal fire prepared for the devil and his angels (Matt. 25:41). The rich man at whose gate lay poor Lazarus is "in agony in this fire," "in this place of torment" (Luke 16:25, 28). Worst of all is the command of the king who has his enemies brought into his presence and killed before his very eyes (Luke 19:27).

We may compare how the passages in the Old Testament that advocated the slaughter of the Canaanites or the slaying of Achan and his entire family have a view of corporate guilt and the necessity for corporate punishment that we undoubtedly would find unacceptable today, but nevertheless these texts bear witness to the divine intolerance of sin and the way in which war and exile were seen as divine judgments upon guilty nations. Other passages in Scripture indicate that people will be punished for their own crimes and not for those of their relatives.

There would be universal agreement among civilized people that no human being should perpetrate horrors of the kind described in the parabolic imagery; those who do so are branded as war criminals and are guilty of crimes against humanity. Even where death sentences are carried out today in "civilized" countries, they apparently are intended to be executed swiftly and comparatively painlessly (although the grim reality may be rather different).

It is incredible that God should so act. So we are alerted to the conclusion that the imagery in the parables is imagery belonging to a time in a society that was accustomed to such things in real life and saw no incongruity in portraying divine judgment in that way. But we can no longer think of God in that way, even if this is imagery used by Jesus. Our basis lies in a mind nurtured by the Spirit, the mind of Christ, which has taught us that such behavior is unacceptable among human beings and that it cannot be justified in the case of God by saying that he is free to act differently from believers. True, we must leave vengeance to God (Rom. 12:19), but that does not mean that he carries out vengeance in this kind of way. For God to be a just judge means precisely that he is *not* like the human tyrants portrayed in the parables. We therefore have to say that while the parables warn of the inescapable reality of divine judgment, their imagery must not be pressed too far.[16]

Why does Jesus teach in this way? I have argued that he had to speak so that the people of his time would understand, and therefore he used the standard imagery of human judgment in a way that would make it as plain as possible that God is utterly opposed to wrong behavior and will judge it perfectly. I suspect that the people of his day were not as aware of the unacceptability of such imagery as we, hopefully, are today. We might compare how small children play games in which they use toy

16. Similar imagery, to be sure, is found in Revelation and elsewhere, but there are good grounds for taking it symbolically and not literally.

guns and pretend to kill people without reflecting on the fact that such behavior in real life is utterly wrong.

As a result of all this we must recognize that in our reading of them, the Gospels sometimes have to be understood on *two levels:* the level of the original hearers of Jesus and the level of Matthew's audience (including ourselves).

A well-known example is the prohibition against evangelizing Gentiles in Matt. 10:5–6. In light of the post-Easter saying within the Gospel itself in Matt. 28:18–20, the standard way of dealing with this text is to say that the prohibition in Matt. 10 is limited in application to the period before the resurrection (cf. the correction of the saying in Luke 10:4 about not carrying a purse, bag, and sandals in Luke 22:35–36). We have some grounds for thinking that post-Easter missionaries can ignore Matt. 10:5–6. Therefore, what looks like authoritative instruction in one part of the book has to be recognized as time-bound in the light of other places. But the matter does not end there, for Matt. 10 as a whole contains teaching about mission that is intended to apply also to the postresurrection period (cf. 10:18). Consequently, there may be other aspects of the mission discourse that no longer apply or have to be modified. Are we at liberty to ignore or reinterpret such aspects without such clear pointers as Matt. 28 provided in this one specific case? Yet, if the chapter as a whole clearly is meant to give guidance to post-Easter missionaries, we surely must be prepared to do so, recognizing that the teaching may have been intended in one sense for pre-Easter missionaries and in another sense for the later situation.

The teaching of Jesus belongs to the liminal period; it is given before the new covenant has been fully inaugurated and uses the imagery of the time. It is legitimate to recognize this and to go beyond it in the directions indicated by the post-Easter revelation. The teaching of Jesus is not set aside; otherwise the church would not have composed and used the Gospels.[17] The Gospels were not simply of historical interest. Their teaching remains authoritative, but we have the broad principle that it

---

17. Perhaps it is worth commenting that some Christians (evangelicals) tend to build their theology and Christian life solely on the Epistles (with a dash of John), while other Christians (liberals) tend to confine themselves to the Synoptic Gospels. Both groups sell themselves short.

is to be understood and extended in the light of the continuing revelation in the post-Easter period. Teaching given in the context of life in Judaism is extended to apply to the church of Jews and Gentiles. Teaching given in the imagery of the time must be reinterpreted appropriately.

In the Early Church

Some further pointers to principles may be found by considering the early church. We will look at some examples of specific developments in the early church and ask whether these provide guidelines for how we may go further.

To a considerable extent progress in doctrine in the early church arises out of the encounter with what was considered to be false teaching and *the need to respond to errors*. Four interlocking things happen here: the identification of error, the appeal to established teaching, the appeal to Christian insight, and the development of doctrine to outflank error.

The Apostolic Tradition

We have seen that errors in doctrine could arise in at least two ways. The fact that prophecies given in church were to be tested (1 Corinthians; 1 John) shows clearly that they were regarded as a potential source of error. Unfortunately, we are not told how the testing was carried out beyond mention of the christological criterion. The other source of error lay in teaching, which evidently was something different from prophecy.

Paul was well aware when false teaching was being given. How did he know that it was wrong? He has a clear concept of *the gospel* and rejects what he perceives to be inconsistent with it. The concept of a fixed tradition, the "apostolic deposit," becomes especially clear in the Pastoral Epistles. The New Testament writers have an understanding that there is such a thing as the faith once and for all delivered to the church, although no one goes so far as to define it in detail. It is my view that despite the differences in expression, this understanding is shared by all the New Testament writers insofar as they give us sufficient evidence to form some idea of their basic theology. The efforts

of scholars from C. H. Dodd onwards to show that the basic
"kerygma" lay at the root of the theology of all the main New
Testament witnesses give us reason to believe that there was a
common core of doctrine that people developed in their own
characteristic ways.

We may regard this basic core as the defining center of
early Christian theology. It became the interpretative key for
Christian theology. If we were to start with the Old Testament
and we did not know about Christ and the New Testament, we
probably would land in rabbinic Judaism and face the post-
A.D. 70 problem of how to cope with guilt and forgiveness in
the absence of sacrifices. Knowledge of Christ and of the basic
Christian understanding of his death provides the leads to an
understanding of the trajectory that runs through the Old Testament. Similarly, the apostolic deposit forms the criterion for
the evaluation of whatever is put forward as Christian teaching
to see whether it is a legitimate and necessary development or
a false and dangerous lead.

The danger, of course, of using Christ, or, as I prefer to say,
the apostolic deposit, as a kind of canon within the canon or
criterion for evaluating its several parts is that it is far too easy
for us to remake Christ and the gospel subjectively in our own
image. It may, therefore, be better to say that we understand the
canon in the light of our own Christian mind and illumination
by the Spirit, and to recognize that this term "our own Christian
mind" uses "our" inclusively to include other Christians past and
present, near and far.

A Mind Nurtured on the Gospel

I have already referred a number of times to the concept of *a
mind nurtured on the gospel*. I have spoken of the way in which
this mind may suggest that we need to develop or go beyond
Scripture at certain points. But is this mind a reliable indicator
of what we are actually to do, and does it constitute any kind
of criterion?

We find evidence for this concept in the New Testament.
There is the teaching of Paul about the guidance of the Spirit
so that people can "speak, not in words taught to us by human
wisdom, but in words taught by the Spirit, expressing spiritual

truths in spiritual words"; he then sums up his point by saying, "We have the mind of Christ" (1 Cor. 2:13, 16). The letter from the apostles and elders after the Jerusalem Council could say, "It seemed good to the Holy Spirit and to us" (Acts 15:28).

This kind of understanding is not confined to Paul and the apostles or church leaders. Spiritual people recognize the truth of Paul's words; the Spirit working in them matches the Spirit inspiring Paul (1 Cor. 2:13–15). Paul assumes that people who are prophets or are spiritually gifted will recognize the truth of what he says (1 Cor. 14:37). Paul prays that believers will receive wisdom and understanding (Eph. 1:17–19), for there is the danger that some people may be unspiritual and unready to receive the teaching given by spiritual people, let alone to give it (1 Cor. 3:1–4). The principle in Phil. 2:2 about being like-minded applies to Christian thinking in general, not just to the practical questions of mutual love and consideration in the church. The continued emphasis in the New Testament on the need for Christians to think for themselves suggests that a wooden acceptance of scriptural teaching is inappropriate.

This would give us a criterion for theological understanding in the nature of a mind that is transformed by sanctification (Rom. 12:2). But it is closely linked to the apostolic deposit. Ephesians 4:20–21 implies that there was a standard of teaching about Christian behavior. It is present in the exhortations and teaching about life in Christ or in the Lord, which take ethical commands and lift them to a higher level.

A Twofold Principle

What we have at work in the New Testament, therefore, is a combination of the apostolic deposit and Spirit-given insight. These two factors work together to detect error and to promote true development in Christian doctrine and practice. The combination of a doctrinal, christological criterion and a renewed mind enables believers to develop the implications of their faith and to come to fresh insights to deal with new knowledge and the danger of false belief. By these means believers were able to assess new revelations by prophets and new teaching of other kinds, and this led to fuller development of doctrine.

One test for prophets was their christological orthodoxy. The tests for valid belief were elaborated from "Jesus Christ is Lord" (1 Cor. 12:3) to "Jesus Christ come in the flesh" as Docetism flourished (1 John 4:2–3). Yet there are people who hold fast to an orthodox interpretation of the person of Jesus and go wildly astray in other ways. Even the tests in 1 John, though they are an advance on 1 Cor. 12, are not infallible, and we may well want to argue for further developments. There is a trajectory here that entitles us to establish even more stringent tests. The later development of creeds and systematic theology is a continuation of this process that can never come to an end, for, to derive a theological corollary from Murphy's Law: one cannot make a body of doctrine heresy-proof, because heretics are so ingenious. One danger at the other extreme is when tests become too stringent, and the niceties of pretribulationism or the like become the test of orthodoxy.

Another familiar development is found in Paul's doctrine of justification, which, in my view, developed as a way of expressing the heart of his theology of salvation that arose out of conflict with Judaizing tendencies. The stress on the supremacy of Christ in Colossians is also a response to erroneous teaching.

In such ways the New Testament writers go beyond the apostolic deposit to combat error and to find *fresh ways of expressing the gospel*. Orthodoxy is not tied to specific vocabularies and forms of words.

Applying the Model

I propose that we have a scriptural model here for development in doctrine after the closing of the canon. We now have the apostolic deposit in Scripture and examples of how different writers devised safeguards against error and developed deeper positive understanding through the interplay of the apostolic deposit and their Spirit-inspired insights. Just as the early church tested the utterances of prophets, so also the church must test the utterances of both its contemporary prophets and its contemporary teachers. But this gives us a basis for the unavoidable task of developing our theology further.

Today we need reasoned Christian responses to new situations, such as scientific discoveries and medical progress, which might be counted as "new teaching." So, for example, a Christian response to abortion or euthanasia or genetic engineering would be an expression of teaching about humanity that goes beyond biblical teaching. In such a situation there would be a new expression of Christian theology that has to be tested specifically for its Christian character in light of Scripture but that is on another level of expression. Clearly, christological orthodoxy alone is inadequate as a test; we would need, in this example, to explore a biblical understanding of humanity.

How does this work out in practice? In some cases the change in expression may not lead to significant differences from what went before. I am, however, specifically concerned with the problems that arise when this process may seem to lead to the relativizing of scriptural teaching.

An example of each from the Pastoral Epistles may be helpful.

Consider *Christology*. Here three things are happening. First, there is the use of the terminology of epiphany for the two comings of Christ with the fresh nuances that this introduces about the revelation of what previously was invisible and the concept of God's saving and helping intervention in the world. Second, there is the way in which the epiphany is not just the coming of Christ, but the whole event in which the grace of God is revealed, including the establishment of the church and the proclamation of the gospel. Third, there is the explicit understanding of Jesus as "our great God and Savior," which is anticipated in Rom. 9:5 but here has become much more a deliberate part of the writer's theology.[18]

These developments are significant because they establish as clearly as possible that the salvation event includes both the coming of the Christ and the proclamation of the gospel, and also that Jesus is our God and Savior in a way that firmly establishes him as the only Savior. They reveal the inadequacy of any Christology that stresses the role of Jesus simply as teacher or as Messiah. Both these points are highly relevant in our contemporary situation. There is a clear trajectory so that we have an unfolding of what was latent and implicit earlier. Specifically,

18. We might compare the developed version of Peter's confession in Matt. 16:16 with his confession in Mark 8:29.

we may go further by emphasizing that if Jesus is "our great God and Savior," then it is impossible to make a separation between him and God the Father as if we could be saved without Jesus, and specifically the Jesus who died for our sins and was raised from the dead. Thus, we have all the stronger basis for the kind of statements made in John 14:6 and Acts 4:12 and for a critique of any suggestions that we need not evangelize Jews, Muslims, and others who do not see the need for Jesus as Savior.

Consider now the more controversial question of *ecclesiology*.[19] The early Pauline understanding of the church as a body is modified in Ephesians and Colossians through the development of the concept of Christ as the head, and this means that the significance of the body metaphor is considerably enlarged and the "center of gravity" shifted as a result. (One could no longer talk in this context of individual Christians being like the nose or the ears.) Here there may be an unfolding of ideas already latent; the relationship of Christ to the church and the supply of his Spirit to it were already expressed in other ways, but they were now made part of this picture of the church.

However, in the Pastoral Epistles the concept of the church as household is developed, and the body metaphor is not used. In 1 Corinthians and Romans the body metaphor emphasizes the mutual ministry and giftedness of the members of the congregation. In the Pastoral Epistles, however, there is more emphasis on the ministry of the leaders, and the ministry of the members is much less prominent (some would say absent). The household metaphor ties in with the idea of a more significant role for leadership as compared with 1 Corinthians. Some would

19. There is the question of whether Paul's thinking developed from less mature to more mature views, although evangelical scholars have been loath to go down that road. For a proposal that Paul's views on the law changed somewhat, and that the earlier ideas in Galatians were developed rather differently in Romans, see J. W. Drane, *Paul: Libertine or Legalist? A Study in the Theology of the Major Pauline Epistles* (London: SPCK, 1975).

It would lead us away from our main topic if we were to enter into the question of whether development can be seen in the teaching (and, behind that, in the mind) of Jesus, such as, for instance, that the incident with the Syrophoenician woman led to a change in his attitude toward Gentiles. Is there evidence of Jesus learning as he went along, or at least receiving further insight from the Father? See J. R. Michaels, *Servant and Son: Jesus in Parable and Gospel* (Atlanta: John Knox, 1981).

argue that the equality of the members in the body metaphor is replaced by the more hierarchical pattern of the household, with its distinctions between old and young and male and female. We have a picture of the congregation in which much is said about the leaders and the teaching that they give, and there is no indication that other members of the congregation were sharing in verbal ministry to any extent.

Now, what do we do with these two accounts? If either is read on its own, we have a somewhat different ethos in the ecclesiology that could have different practical results. What sort of ecclesiology would result from knowing 1 Timothy but not 1 Corinthians, as may have been the situation for at least some readers? For those of us who know the texts representing the body metaphor and the household metaphor, here are four possibilities:

1. We have two incompatible understandings of the nature of the congregation. The temptation then is to emphasize the differences, even the incompatibility between them. People then may be free to adopt either one or the other of these understandings or neither of them. We might consider this to be the liberal option.[20]

2. We are to see a development in which the later and final form supersedes the other, and therefore churches must follow the Pastoral Epistles. That is roughly the traditional Roman Catholic position. Again, it represents a rejection of one pattern in favor of another, or at least a preference for the later pattern.[21]

3. In 1 Corinthians we see the heart of the New Testament, and the Pastoral Epistles represent a later fossilization, and therefore we should get back to the "center" of the New Testament, namely, to Paul. Charismatics may take this line without consciously recognizing what they are doing.

4. Rather than seeing the Pastoral Epistles as the end of a development (and therefore setting out a necessary pattern of church leadership and ministry in terms of overseers and dea-

20. It is typified by E. Käsemann, who tended to reject whatever in the New Testament was not truly Pauline.

21. The Catholic is no more likely than the evangelical to deliberately reject part of Scripture.

cons), we should hold together the teaching of 1 Corinthians and the Pastoral Epistles in a fruitful tension, recognizing that at various times one or the other requires more emphasis. The lesson of the New Testament is that there was diversity and that we should learn from the different contingent applications. Some interpreters, like myself, tend to play down the differences and to see little or no dissimilarity in principle between them, whereas others see greater differences between them. For example, E. E. Lemcio says that we have two diverse models of the church in 1 Corinthians and the Pastoral Epistles and that we must use dialectic in our interpretation.[22] I take it that he means by this that we must somehow hold the two texts in balance. Each must be allowed to correct and balance the other. On both views there is validity in each of the scriptural passages, and if they cannot be harmonized fully, then we can profit from the tensions. This implies that neither one is sufficient on its own. Similarly, I would deal in this same manner with the problems caused by 1 Cor. 14:34–35 and 1 Tim. 2:8–15 rather than argue that these passages must be decisive over other passages.

This raises the question of whether a principle of this kind may lead to the relativization of some teaching. If the tendency in the Pastoral Epistles was to restrict ministry to the leadership (from which women were excluded), then clearly in a situation where false teaching is not the problem that it was back then and where a congregation is better educated in the faith (thanks to the ready availability of Scripture, Christian books, and Christian education), we are not tied to the scenario in the Pastoral Epistles, and I have no difficulties with saying this with regard to 1 Tim. 2. Here, I believe, is a passage that certainly was authoritative as a measure to be applied in the difficult situation in the church at that time wherein a constellation of problems required a solution that involved the barring of women from teaching. However, none of the reasons adduced for that solution require that this be a barrier for all times and places, and therefore I do not think that the practical conclusion drawn there is a permanent one.

22. E. E. Lemcio, "Images of the Church in 1 Corinthians and 1 Timothy: An Exercise in Canonical Hermeneutics," *Asbury Theological Journal* 56 (2001): 45–59.

The principle that I am proposing, then, is this: we should take our guidance for our continuing interpretation of Scripture and the development of theology from what goes on in Scripture itself:

1. *The early Christian rereading of the Old Testament took place in light of the new covenant inaugurated by Jesus Christ, and we must read the Old Testament similarly.* There must be a Christian understanding of the Old Testament when it comes to the question of how we appropriate it for Christian use. This does not exclude but rather requires the most careful exegesis of the texts in their original settings and in their canonical context in the Old Testament as Jewish Scripture, but it insists that that is not the last word. The new covenant forces us to a consideration of the continuity and discontinuity with the old covenant and to the clear recognition that what once was authoritative for the people of God is no longer authoritative in the same way for the new people of God. Some vital teaching remains valid, but other parts must be understood differently.

2. *The teaching of Jesus must be understood in light of his death and resurrection and the apostolic teaching.* His teaching was given in a liminal period and must be taken up into the fuller post-Easter revelation. Since it was addressed mainly to Jews and used the imagery of the time, it may not be adequate or appropriate for a different audience.

3. *The teaching of the apostles and their colleagues took place on the basis of a combination of the "word" and the insights given by the Spirit.* We also must understand and use their teaching as we seek to be faithful to the Lord and the gospel in our own time by holding fast to the apostolic deposit and understanding and applying it under the continuing guidance of the Spirit.

Working in this way, we affirm the ongoing supreme authority of Scripture, but we recognize that Scripture needs interpretation and fresh application, both in our doctrine and in our practice. We do our theology, both academic and practical, in light of the gospel as the essential core of biblical teaching and by the use of minds that are continually nourished by the gospel and renewed by the Spirit. Changing situations and changing culture may alert us to the ongoing need for reconsideration of our belief and practice, but the factors that control our thinking must always be the gospel and the Christian mind that is

shaped by it. Since we may be led to conclude that some teachings of Scripture need to be understood and applied differently
from in the first century, it follows that such reconsideration is
a task that involves considerable risk, but also great is the risk
of misleading the church by dwelling in the first century and
refusing to go beyond the letter of Scripture. We must beware
of the danger of failing to understand what God is saying to his
people today and muzzling his voice.[23] Scripture itself constrains
us to the task of ongoing theological development.

Conclusion

Here I present seven points that I hope to have established:

1. There is development in doctrine throughout the Bible
leading to diversity and greater maturity in teaching at different
stages, although the later is not necessarily more mature than
the earlier.

2. There is an incompleteness in Scripture, seen in factors
such as the diversity, the occasional nature of the teaching, and
the impossibility of dealing with later questions and problems,
all of which mean that doctrine can and must develop beyond
scriptural statements.

3. Since the revelation is given not simply in individual texts
as units of meaning, but through the whole of Scripture, the individual texts must be seen in light of the whole, and some may
be seen as staging posts on the way to fuller understanding; they
are no longer valid in their original form, although they were
once authoritative in that form, but continue to be authoritative
in a different way.

4. There is continuity throughout the process. The God of
the Old Testament is the same God as in the New Testament
and acts in essentially the same ways. Likewise, the teaching
of Jesus stands in continuity with the Old Testament and the

---

23. In an unpublished paper in defense of Today's New International Version,
D. A. Carson insists that a gender-inclusive translation of the Bible runs the risk
of not always getting it right, but a noninclusive translation that takes no risks
faces significant dangers in failing to communicate the actual sense of Scripture
to contemporary people.

teaching of the early church; and within the developments in the early church there is a firm understanding of the "gospel" as a given.

5. The development is controlled by various principles: the shift from the old covenant to the new covenant; the shift from the liminal period to the early church;[24] the facing of new situations, new currents of thought, new errors, and the like.

6. Developments in doctrine and new understandings after the closing of the canon are inevitable. These must be based on continuity with the faith once given to God's people, and must be in accordance with what I have called "the mind of Christ." They may relativize some aspects of biblical teaching that was appropriate for specific occasions and cultural settings or where the gospel itself (and not some modern or postmodern agenda) requires us to do so.

7. In this way we affirm the ongoing supreme authority of Scripture, but we recognize that Scripture needs interpretation and fresh application, both in our doctrine and in our practice.

24. I should emphasize that the boundaries must not be drawn too tightly. The period of the early church is itself in some respects a liminal period as the apostolic teaching develops and early Christians work out its implications.

4

Into the Great "Beyond"

A Theologian's Response
to the Marshall Plan

Kevin J. Vanhoozer
Trinity Evangelical Divinity School

Introduction

It gives me great pleasure to respond to the preceding chapters, both to their author and to their topic. Professor Marshall has been a faithful laborer in the vineyard for decades, training two generations of New Testament scholars. North American students in particular have gone into the far country in order to work with him. If I. Howard will not come to the mountain, the mountain must go to I. Howard. . . .

I did not go to Aberdeen for my Ph.D., but I was awakened from my hermeneutical slumbers some twenty-five years ago by a book that Howard edited: *New Testament Interpretation: Essays on Principles and Methods*. Already in that book he was saying that New Testament interpretation "reaches its goal only when it examines the meaning of the text for today."[1] And he notes in the introduction that a concern for exposition and for the present-day reader may take us "beyond the original intention" of the biblical authors.[2]

Let me suggest that we approach this question—what it means to be biblical in our exposition—not with Lessing's famous metaphor of the "ugly ditch" that separates biblical studies and systematic theology, but with the more hopeful metaphor of the "chunnel." The chunnel—the tunnel dug under the English Channel—is a most impressive engineering project. The British bored one way and the French another, and they met, thanks to sophisticated global positioning instruments and the like, exactly in the middle. That is the image we are after: exegetes from Aberdeen and Tyndale House chunnelling toward the Continent, the land of systematic theology, and systematicians chunneling toward the exegetes from their own side.

Where will exegetes and systematicians meet? On the fertile ground of the theological interpretation of Scripture, defined as "that practice whereby theological concerns and interests inform and are informed by a reading of scripture."[3] This chunnel has, of course, been dug before. Before there was an ugly ditch separating biblical studies from theology, biblical interpreters in the early, medieval, and Reformation church were reading Scripture prayerfully and reflectively in order better to know and love God.

Marshall defines exposition as "understanding what the text may be saying to contemporary readers as opposed to original readers." To exposit is to set forth or interpret. Exposition may well be the place where the biblical and theological chunnels meet. As Karl Barth well knew, what makes theology necessary is the task of preaching, of reflecting on how it is possible to proclaim, "Thus saith the Lord." Exegesis and theology are the

---

1. I. Howard Marshall, ed., *New Testament Interpretation: Essays on Principles and Methods* (Grand Rapids: Eerdmans, 1977), 8.

2. Ibid., 14.

3. Stephen Fowl, ed., *The Theological Interpretation of Scripture: Classic and Contemporary Readings* (Oxford: Blackwell, 1997), xiii.

crucial guardrails against "impository" preaching, whereby the interpreter imposes his or her own notions onto the text. Marshall's search for a *principled* way of expositing the Scriptures for today is therefore to be commended.

The Argument: Contours of the "Marshall Plan"

Although there is much in these chapters that is descriptive, I take it that Marshall's ultimate aim is prescriptive; hence his plea for a "principled" approach. Let us call the main prescription—to develop theology as does the Bible itself, that is, with *biblical* principles—the "Marshall plan."

Marshall's chapter 1 is largely preliminary to his main proposal, but it is nonetheless helpful for that. There are still a few pockets of exegetical resistance in the evangelical world to the very notion of hermeneutics. Some biblical scholars may still harbor the suspicion, indelibly imprinted on my memory in the form of a remark by a Tyndale House doctoral student in New Testament, that hermeneutical mumbo-jumbo is simply an excuse for avoiding the question of the Bible's truth. The startled response that I gave then is one that, on further reflection, I still believe: the question of meaning logically precedes the question of truth. One cannot make a judgment as to a text's truth until one has first determined what it is saying/claiming. Determining the literary genre of Scripture is of paramount importance. Nevertheless, I am sympathetic to the concern that we not avoid responding to Scripture because we are so busy interpreting it. In my view, hermeneutics is not an excuse for deferring faith and obedience, but is the precondition for a genuinely faithful and obedient response.

Evangelical biblical scholars have excelled above all in what Marshall calls the second level of study: specific exegetical *procedures*. Indeed, at times it seems that evangelicals simply collapse the first and the third levels, general hermeneutics and application respectively, into the second. The net result is that biblical interpretation becomes a matter of what Gadamer calls "method" only. Who needs prayer when we have a library from Aland to Zerwick on the shelf, a syntactical concordance of the Greek New Testament on the hard drive, and a ten-step approach to diagramming sentences in our head? My impression is that evangelical biblical scholars are adept in using the latest linguistic "technology." The problem, however, is that much more is required to interpret the Bible than a knowledge of grammar and vocabulary. Seminaries do their students (and the churches in which they preach) a disservice to the extent that they focus on linguistic studies to the detriment, if not exclusion, of theological interpretation, exposition, and application.

Professor Marshall then turns to the challenge of application and appropriation. In chapter 2 Marshall considers two contrasting approaches to the use of Scripture in ethics, worship, and theology. He gives several examples, but as a whole the section consists of variations on a theme, namely, the choice between conservative/progressive approaches (which Marshall styles in terms of a contrast between two mentalities, the "Puritan regulative" and the "Anglican normative"). What emerges from this survey is the need for a principle to guide and govern development beyond Scripture. But where does this further principle come from, and is *it* biblical? Wretched expositor that I am! Who will deliver me from this infinite hermeneutical regress?

After being shown that there is development of doctrine within the Bible itself, we get a first formulation of the Marshall plan, expressed in the form of an intuition: we need to mine Scripture itself for principles that enable us to go beyond Scripture. The crucial move is made at the end of chapter 2: the closing of the canon is not incompatible with the nonclosing, or openness, of the interpretation of the canon. The key is to go *beyond* the Bible *biblically*.

In chapter 3 Marshall searches for this key, mining the canon for biblical patterns and principles for going beyond previous Scripture that the church can follow today. Specifically, he adduces three biblical principles for going beyond the Bible.

First, the Christian interpretation of the Old Testament took place in light of the new covenant situation inaugurated by Jesus Christ.

Second, Jesus' teaching was given "between the times," as it were, and itself must be understood in light of post-Easter apostolic preaching. This "liminal" period limits the appropriateness of some of Jesus' teaching (this point may occasion some weeping and gnashing of teeth from Bible publishers when they realize what it means for their red-letter editions!). I wish to comment further on this second principle before moving on to discuss the third.

Marshall contends that Jesus' teaching is relativized by his Jewish and cultural context, *and* by his position in redemption history. The bulk of Jesus' teaching comes before the resurrection, before Pentecost, and thus before the Spirit's ministry of the new covenant. I see no problem in the notion that Jesus' Christology (so to speak) was underdeveloped; the disciples would not have understood it on the hither side of the resurrection. But I am a bit troubled when Marshall appeals to the liminal period in order to relativize Jesus' doctrine of God.

Marshall believes that some of the images that Jesus uses to depict divine judgment are inappropriate for our time: "It is incredible that God should so act. . . . We can no longer think of God in that way, even if this is imagery used by Jesus." Is that really so? I am not that sanguine about this. After all, God is no tame lion.

Marshall wants Christians to get "beyond" genocide. So do I. But I am not prepared to say that God's judgment of the world, or of nations, is "intrinsically wrong" if it involves killing people. Marshall is doing more than "reconsidering," it seems to me, when he says that we "can no longer think of God in that way." Unless we are prepared to jettison significant portions of the Old Testament (or to revise their meaning in the light of contemporary sensitivities), this way of going beyond Scripture has more of Marcion than of Marshall about it. For it really is not about numbers. If Marshall is to be consistent, he should say that God does not have the right to take a single life. After all, that is unacceptable human behavior, and we cannot justify God "by saying that he is free to act differently from believers." On the contrary, I think we must say that God is indeed free to act differently from believers. The Creator is bound not by the laws that he has imposed upon creation, but by his own nature. To confuse God's love with our culturally conditioned imitations is to go beyond the Bible not biblically, but culturally. Finally, if we are shocked by images of judgment, what are we to make of the cross? Even after the fervent prayers of a righteous man in a garden in Gethsemane, the Father did not remove the cup of judgment.

It strikes me that Marshall is bringing an already developed doctrine of God (and an understanding of the gospel) to the exegetical table. His comment that we "can no longer think of God that way" reminds me of a similar statement, made by James Barr, that we "cannot" believe that God reveals himself in Scripture: "Today I think we believe, or have to believe, that God's communication with the men of the biblical period was not on any different terms from the mode of his communication with his people today."[4] But why, we may ask, do we *have* to believe these things about God, especially when the Bible presents God as a speaker and as a judge?[5] Marshall himself is aware that "something more than exegesis is involved." And that brings us to the next point.

The third of Marshall's biblical principles for doctrinal development is to understand the apostolic teaching in light of the total revelation of the gospel. Here he invokes the notions of "minds nurtured on the gospel" and "the mind of Christ" (though with regard to the latter one might be inclined to ask whether Jesus' mind was sufficiently nurtured on the gospel, given the violent imagery he sometimes used when speaking of God!). This is as close as Marshall comes to articulating his own principle, and to my mind it bears a close resemblance to William Webb's "redemptive trajectory" approach, about which I will have something to say below.[6]

Theological Table Talk: Comments and Concerns

Marshall's chapters represent an encouraging initiative toward a proper dialogue between exegetes and systematicians. Their two disciplines have become so specialized that such bilateral discussions are rare indeed because so few practitioners are, as

4. James Barr, *The Bible in the Modern World* (London: SCM, 1973), 17–18.

5. It should not go unnoticed that the Gospels were written not during the liminal period, but after the resurrection, and probably *after* Paul's epistles. This minor chronological point has, I think, a major effect on Marshall's assumption about the "in between" nature of Jesus' teaching.

6. William J. Webb, *Slaves, Women, and Homosexuals: Exploring the Hermeneutics of Cultural Analysis* (Downers Grove, Ill.: InterVarsity, 2001). Marshall notes that a similar approach was employed by R. T. France.

it were, bilingual. This is deeply regrettable. One of the main merits of Marshall's work is its desire to return biblical studies to the fold of the theological disciplines.

Bible, Doctrine, Theology

What might the first three chapters of the present book have looked like if they had been written by a theologian—by me, for example? In the first place, the bibliography would be different. Marshall states that less attention has been given to the question of how theology develops from the Bible than has been given to ethics. That is not my perception of the matter. A number of recent works address the matter explicitly.[7] At the same time, even if Marshall had read all these books—and perhaps he has!—he still with some justification might be able to say, "I have looked in vain for a principled way of moving from Bible to doctrine."

A second difference concerns the use of the term "doctrine." Marshall uses it as if we all agreed what it meant. Yet theologians have been debating this in earnest for the past twenty years or so, roughly since the publication of George Lindbeck's *The Nature of Doctrine*.[8] Are doctrines informative truth claims or propositions about objective realities (the traditional view), or are they articulations of human feelings and experiences set forth in speech (Schleiermacher)? Or are they intersubjective grammatical rules for church language and church life (Lindbeck's own "cultural-linguistic" view)? Clearly, if the aim is to develop doctrine from Scripture, one first has to decide what doctrine is.

My own view is that doctrine is direction for the church's fitting participation in the ongoing drama of redemption.[9] Doctrine

7. For example, David Kelsey, *Proving Doctrine: The Uses of Scripture in Modern Theology* (Harrisburg, Pa: Trinity, 1999); Gerald O'Collins and Daniel Kendall, *The Bible for Theology: Ten Principles for the Theological Use of Scripture* (New York: Paulist Press, 1997); Alister McGrath, *The Genesis of Doctrine: A Study in the Foundation of Doctrinal Criticism* (Grand Rapids: Eerdmans, 1997); Jaroslav Pelikan, *The Development of Doctrine: Some Historical Prolegomena* (New Haven: Yale University Press, 1969).

8. George Lindbeck, *The Nature of Doctrine: Religion and Theology in a Post-liberal Age* (Philadelphia: Westminster, 1984).

9. I argue this at length in *The Drama of Doctrine: A Canonical-Linguistic Approach to Theology* (Louisville: Westminster John Knox, 2004).

has a cognitive component, for we must understand what God has done in Christ for our salvation (and this includes getting the identity of the divine dramatis personae right), but the thrust of Christian doctrine is not mere knowledge, but rather wisdom: we demonstrate our understanding by speaking and acting in manners that correspond to reality as it is disclosed by (and being conformed to) Jesus Christ. Although I cannot pursue the point here, I believe that this understanding of doctrine yields a *theodramatic* principle for continuing (I won't say "going beyond") Scripture in new contexts.[10]

A third difference between Marshall's approach and mine would be a greater concern for metaphorical precision and conceptual analysis. In particular, I have in mind the metaphor of "going beyond" and the concept of "development." It is to this metaphor and concept that I devote the rest of my response.

George Lakoff and Mark Johnson examine what they call "spatial" metaphors in their book *Metaphors We Live By*. We speak of "high" standards, or of putting one's feelings "aside."[11] These spatial metaphors give us a way to conceive nonspatial relations. "Beyond" is a remarkably elastic spatial preposition. The *Oxford English Dictionary* offers "outside the range of," "at the further side of," and "more than" as possible definitions. (It also reminds us that as a noun, the "beyond" refers to the unknown after death.)

Doctrine clearly goes "beyond" Scripture. But how, exactly? Does a simple change of wording constitute a case of going "beyond"? Marshall notes that neither word in the term "penal substitution" is strictly biblical. Nor, for that matter, is "Trinity." Is this a change of wording or of concept? Does every translation go "beyond"? What does "development beyond" really mean? Minimally, Marshall speaks of clarifying what is already "in" Scripture. Yet some developments do more than clarify; they revise or even discard biblical teaching and go on to postulate something that is not even implicitly in Scripture. How can we go "beyond" without going too far, without going beyond the pale?

10. "Going beyond," then, will be primarily a matter of achieving theodramatic rather than logical consistency with Scripture.

11. George Lakoff and Mark Johnson, *Metaphors We Live By* (Chicago: University of Chicago Press, 1980), 16–17.

We can construe the two approaches to the use of Scripture in ethics, worship, and theology in terms of "binding and loosing." To invoke Matt. 16:19 in this context is apt, for Jesus' teaching (which probably is not for the liminal period only) concerns the locus of authority. "Binding" and "loosing" are rabbinic terms that have to do with "forbidding" and "permitting." This is precisely Marshall's point: when are developments beyond Scripture permitted, and when are they not? To know the answer to *that* question is to hold the keys of the kingdom of theology. I propose to focus in the remainder of this response on four possible ways of "going beyond" Scripture biblically.

Going Beyond: Extrabiblical Conceptualities

Let us consider, in the first instance, the use of technical terms and concepts not found in Scripture. Does the doctrine of the Trinity, with its notion of *homoousios* and three "persons," go "beyond" Scripture? Is every change in vocabulary a development "beyond" Scripture?

John Calvin had to confront this objection, namely, that theology imposes "foreign words" upon the text. In book 1, chapter 13, of the *Institutes*, this reader of Scripture, this most biblical of theologians, defends the development of a technical terminology to express doctrinal truths on the grounds that they *aid* the interpretation of Scripture. Calvin writes, "But what prevents us from explaining in clearer words those matters in Scripture which perplex and hinder our understanding, yet which conscientiously and faithfully serve the truth of Scripture itself?"[12] We must not find fault with what renders the truth of Scripture plain and clear. Another advantage of technical concepts is their usefulness in exposing false teaching. Calvin demonstrates this point in regards to Arius: "Say 'consubstantial' and you will tear off the mask of this turncoat, and yet you add nothing to Scripture."[13]

Calvin is advocating an innocuous form of "going beyond" Scripture that is ultimately a matter not of adding anything to its content, but only of rendering what is implicit *explicit*. This first sense of going beyond, then, amounts to no more than

12. *Institutes* 1.13.3.
13. Ibid., 1.13.5.

conceptual clarification. If I may paraphrase Luther: *The biblical interpreter must be a most free lord of all concepts yet subject to none, and a most dutiful servant of the Scriptures, subject to all.*

Going Beyond: Redemptive Trajectories

The redemptive trajectory approach, the second strategy that I wish to consider, is more progressive by contrast. Marshall mentions Webb's important contribution in this regard. The idea is that we discern a redemptive trajectory or spirit-movement component of meaning in certain texts that encourages us to apply the transcultural spirit rather than the culture-bound letter of the text. What lies at the end of this redemptive trajectory? An "ultimate ethic" that may go beyond certain cultural patterns in biblical times and beyond certain cultural patterns in our time. For example, applying the redemptive spirit of the New Testament texts should lead us to eliminate slavery, even though it is not explicitly condemned in Scripture. This is a clear example of movement "beyond" the text.

On this view, the biblical texts are on a trajectory aiming at love, justice, and equality, though not all texts have arrived there yet. One problem with this approach is that the interpreter has to assume that he or she is standing at the end of the trajectory, or at least further along (or better at plotting line slope intercept formulas!), than some of the biblical authors in order to see where it leads. Webb, for his part, thinks that it leads toward racial reconciliation and toward egalitarianism between men and women, but he does not believe that it is so inclusive as to permit homosexual relations. And yet others, such as Luke Johnson and Stephen Fowl, appeal to the very same logic of redemptive trajectory in order to legitimate same-sex relations. Just as the early Christians discerned the redemptive trajectory of the Spirit in the Gentiles in Acts 15, so we should detect the Spirit's work in the lives of homosexual Christians, thus leading us to be more inclusive.[14] The redemptive movement of the text is, on this view, the Spirit of truth who sets free by breaking cultural taboos. The Episcopal Church in America has just ordained its first openly gay bishop,

14. So Stephen E. Fowl, *Engaging Scripture: A Model for Theological Interpretation* (Oxford: Blackwell, 1998), chapter 4.

and other mainline churches are hoping that this particular "redemptive trajectory" will pick up locomotive momentum. Webb admits, "Finding the underlying spirit of a text is a delicate matter."[15] Can one decide what counts as redemptive movement without pretending to stand at the end of the process, without claiming to know what kind of eschatological world the Spirit is creating? Can one go beyond Scripture via the redemptive trajectory approach and at the same time prevent one's own view of the trajectory from lording it over the text? For my own part, I am happier to speak of a christological trajectory, of a movement that leads to the wisdom of God summed up in Jesus Christ, not to something beyond it, even when that something is associated with the Spirit.[16]

Going Beyond: Divine Discourse

Nicholas Wolterstorff's *Divine Discourse* represents yet a third way of going beyond the Bible. Wolterstorff sees the Bible as human discourse that has been divinely appropriated. It is not enough to read for the original human author's intent; rather, we must employ a "second hermeneutic" in order to understand the divine authorial discourse. One principle is that the correct context of any sentence in the Bible is the entire canonical context, the extended divine discourse. Only in light of the whole canonical context can we tell what God is saying in any one part.

Wolterstorff introduces the concept of transitive discourse to illustrate how God can do new things with human discourse. In transitive discourse, by saying one thing we can say or do another thing. For example, when Nathan told King David the story about a rich man taking the lamb of a poor man, he was also accusing David of stealing Uriah's wife. God does something

---

15. Webb, *Slaves, Women, and Homosexuals*, 53.

16. Two further points: First, Webb argues like those who contend for a "justice trajectory" hermeneutic of the U.S. Constitution. In debates about Constitutional interpretation, such a hermeneutic is a useful tool to "get beyond" the intentions of the original framers. Second, I believe that the church is in the same redemptive-historical position as was the early church. James McClendon calls this the "baptist vision": "the present Christian community is the primitive community and the eschatological community" (*Systematic Theology* [2 vols.; Nashville: Abingdon, 1986], 1:31).

similar with the human discourse of Scripture. By appropriating the human discourse of the Song of Songs, which is an ode
to love between man and woman, the divine author tells a story
about, say, the love of Christ for the church.

Wolterstorff's fundamental principle is that interpreters take the
stance and content of God's appropriating discourse to be that of the
human author's appropriated discourse "unless there is good reason
to do otherwise."[17] But among the good reasons to think that God
means something other than what the human authors meant are
our convictions about what God would or would not have intended
to say by appropriating just these texts. Where do *these* convictions
come from? Does not Scripture become a wax nose, a word held
hostage by the vagaries of human belief about God?

We cannot do full justice to Wolterstorff's response to the "wax
nose anxiety." Suffice it to say that Wolterstorff appeals to the
Christian consensus that God never speaks falsehood or says
things that are incompatible with the law of love.

Going Beyond: Continuing Canonical Practices

Let me now turn to a fourth and final way of going beyond
the Bible to develop doctrine biblically: following canonical
practices. This should not be confused with "principlizing"—the
process of extracting timeless principles from their original contexts in Scripture and applying them elsewhere.[18] Three caveats
apply. First, what we see as transcultural principles are in fact
often contaminated by our own cultural biases. Second, too
strong an emphasis on principles tends to privilege didactic passages of Scripture. Third, it is dangerous to think that a set of
deculturalized principles is a more accurate indication of God's
will than its canonical expression.[19]

There is, I think, a better way of directing the church today
while at the same time recognizing the Bible itself, rather than

17. Nicholas Wolterstorff, *Divine Discourse: Philosophical Reflections on the
Claim That God Speaks* (Cambridge: Cambridge University Press, 1995), 204.

18. For the following critique of principlizing I am indebted to David K.
Clark, *To Know and Love God: Method for Theology* (Wheaton, Ill.: Crossway,
2003), 91–98.

19. Clark suggests that Webb's redemptive trajectory approach is a sophisticated version of principlizing (*To Know and Love God*, 94).

some set of decontextualized principles or extratextual trajectory, as authoritative. Doctrine directs the church to speak and act in new situations (e.g., "beyond the Bible") biblically by cultivating what I will call "the mind of the canon." That to which theologians must attend in Scripture is not the words and concepts so much as the *patterns of judgment*. Christian doctrine describes a pattern of judgment present in the biblical texts. To make a judgment is to form an opinion about some thing or to make an assessment about some situation. I agree with David Yeago that *the same judgment can be rendered in a variety of conceptual terms.*[20]

The judgment about Christ that Nicea rendered in terms of *homoousion*, for example, went beyond what Phil. 2 says about Christ's "equality with God." The concepts of Nicea are not those of Philippians. Yet the judgment—what is predicated about the subject Christ—is the same. Doctrine concerns judgments, not concepts. We move from Bible to doctrine not by systematizing Scripture's concepts, nor by extracting (e.g., decontextualizing) principles, but rather by discerning and continuing a pattern of judgment rendered in a variety of linguistic, literary, and conceptual forms.

This leads me to the role of canonical practices and to the importance of canonical competence. Embedded in the canon are the patterns for correct speaking and thinking about God, patterns of judging that represent nothing less than the substance of "sound doctrine." Expositors of Scripture must be apprentices of its diverse canonical practices, participants in "the society of biblical literature." They must learn to read particular texts in the context of the whole of Scripture, and in relation to the center of Scripture, the gospel of Jesus Christ. They must learn not simply to parse the verbs or to process the information, but to render the same kind of judgments as those embedded in the canon in new contexts and with different concepts. "Canon is key: as its name is, so is its nature. 'Rule' is its name, and 'authority' is with it" (cf. 1 Sam. 25:25).

According to Luke 24, it was Jesus himself who taught his disciples to go beyond the Scriptures in order to see how they

---

20. David Yeago, "The New Testament and the Nicene Dogma," in Fowl, ed., *Theological Interpretation of Scripture*, 93.

point to him. Here is a canonical practice—figural reading—that proceeds from Christ's very own prophetic office! As with all the other canonical practices, the point is to train us to see, think, and judge so that we will be fit participants in the ongoing drama of redemption. Canonical practices are rule-governed forms of covenantal behavior that direct the seeing, judging, and acting of the believing community.[21] We acquire canonical competence—a mind nurtured on the Christ-centered canon—when we learn how to make the same kind of judgments about God, the world, and ourselves as those embedded in Scripture.

To exposit the Scriptures is to participate in the canonical practices—practices that form, inform, and transform our speaking, thinking, and living. To interpret the Bible in this manner is to make the church itself an exposition, or what Paul calls a "spectacle" (*theatron*) to the world (1 Cor. 4:9). This theatrical metaphor highlights the pastoral, and practical, function of doctrine. Doctrine, I submit, is an aid for understanding the *theodrama*—what God has done in Jesus Christ. As such, doctrine provides direction for our fitting participation in the ongoing drama of redemption. It is the canonical script that guides the church's performance of the way, the truth, and the life. To be sure, we are not called simply to repeat old formulas, but to embody biblical judgments in new conceptual terms and new cultural contexts.

Note that this final strategy for going beyond the Bible biblically preserves the best of the other approaches. With Calvin, I recognize that new concepts serve biblical judgments. With the redemptive trajectory approach, I recognize that there is movement within Scripture, though I insist that the focus is Christ and therefore erect a canonical fence around the gospel lest the gospel be taken captive by other ideological interests. Finally, with Wolterstorff, I agree that we must treat the canon as the collected works of the divine author, and thus as the necessary context for discovering the Word of God to the church today.

---

21. The canonical practices are ultimately works of the Holy Spirit, the one whose speaking in the canonical Scriptures is the ultimate norm for theology. Acquiring canonical competence is a matter of the Spirit ministering the Word, and hence a means and matter of spiritual formation. I treat these issues at greater length in my *Drama of Doctrine*.

Conclusion: "A Mind Nurtured by the Christ-Centered Canon"

I read this Marshall plan, unlike its namesake of half a century ago, not as a justification of the status quo but as a summons to revolution. Revolutions, in politics and in thought, often begin with questions that, once asked, cannot be forgotten. Professor Marshall has posed a revolutionary question: *Can we go beyond the Bible to get to theology biblically?* Just as revolutionary is its implication that we must storm the academic Bastille that keeps exegetes and theologians imprisoned in separate cells and set the prisoners free to talk and work with one another. We must respond to this challenge of expositing Scripture, in something like the way Marshall indicates, or we will be remiss in our responsibilities and fail in our vocations. In this response I have affirmed the broad outline—the principle!—of the Marshall plan, while at the same time qualifying its "mind nurtured on the gospel" with a "mind nurtured by Christ-centered canonical practices."

Have we met in the middle? I sincerely hope that exegetes and theologians will meet somewhere before they cross over into Jordan. Let us hope, pray, and work for a new chunnel, or better, a new passageway that makes straight in the desert of criticism a highway for the theological interpretation of Scripture (cf. Isa. 40:3). In the meantime, let us make every effort so to be nurtured on the Christ-centered canon that we become expositor-performers who not only interpret, but also live out, the way, the truth, and the life to the glory of God. I applaud Professor I. Howard Marshall for tackling the key issue, for pushing the exegetical envelope, and for seeking a way to recover the "auld alliance" between biblical studies and theology. May his plan prosper, and may his clan increase!

5

Hermeneutics, Biblical Interpretation, and Theology

Hunch, Holy Spirit, or Hard Work?

Stanley E. Porter
McMaster Divinity College

Introduction

The goal of this essay appears to be a simple and straightforward one.[1] I am to marshal a response to the three Hayward Lectures delivered at Acadia Divinity College by Professor

I wish to thank Acadia Divinity College and its principal, Dr. Lee Martin McDonald, for the invitation to be a part of the Hayward Lectures by offering this response to the lectures of the principal speaker, Professor I. Howard Marshall. I also wish to thank my good friend Dr. Craig Evans for his kind hospitality during my time in Wolfville, Nova Scotia.
1. The delivery of the original lecture was not nearly so simple or straightforward. Even though I had been sent the lectures by Professor Marshall in

I. Howard Marshall of the University of Aberdeen under the title "Interpreting the Bible and the Development of Theology." Those who were present for the lectures were offered a rare treat. I think it is fair to say that students, faculty, and staff probably had not had the benefit of hearing this kind of mature Christian reflection on such an important topic in quite some time, if ever. I have known Professor Marshall for nearly twenty years, and he probably would be the last to say what an important occasion these lectures represent for their recipients. I am sure that Professor Marshall is honored to have been asked to deliver the Hayward Lectures for this year, but whatever honor it does him, the greater honor is to this institution that he agreed to come and speak to Acadia Divinity College.

When Professor Marshall speaks about interpreting the Bible and how this relates to the development of Christian theology, he draws upon nearly half a century of important work that he has done in these areas. Much of Professor Marshall's career spanned the second half of last century, which was a very important one especially in the development of evangelical theology in the British context. Professor Marshall is a member of what might be called the second generation of British or British-based New Testament scholars who were fundamental in vitalizing and then revitalizing an evangelical approach to biblical studies in the United Kingdom. This vitalization had a tremendous impact upon evangelical scholarship throughout the world, including North America.

The doyen of evangelical biblical scholarship in the United Kingdom, at least as far as New Testament studies are concerned, was Professor F. F. Bruce, first of the University of Aberdeen (where he was a student and honored with a D.D.), then of the University of Sheffield (my university, where he was first head of the department and then professor, 1947–59), and then of Manchester University (where he was Rylands Professor of Biblical Criticism and Exegesis from 1959 until his retirement in 1978).[2] With the support and affiliation of organizations such as the Tyndale Fellowship (which is part of the Universities and Col-

---

advance, I offered my "response" in October, whereas his lectures were not delivered until November.

2. Professor Bruce also graduated from Cambridge University with a M.A., attended the University of Vienna, and taught at Edinburgh University and the University of Leeds.

leges Christian Fellowship, the British equivalent of InterVarsity Fellowship), Professor Bruce (along with a few others, such as the great Baptist scholar George Beasley-Murray) influenced an entire generation and more of biblical scholars through his voluminous writing and publication, his supervision of numerous doctoral students from all over the world, and his editing of publications such as the *Evangelical Quarterly* (1949–80). Professor Bruce is the only clearly evangelical scholar listed in the recent *Historical Handbook of Major Biblical Interpreters*[3] in the category of twentieth-century European interpreters.

Professor Marshall is a member of the next generation of evangelical New Testament scholars who have picked up the torch from Bruce; they include scholars such as John Drane, Richard France, and Anthony Thiselton (my teacher). Professor Marshall was educated at the University of Aberdeen (M.A., B.D., Ph.D.),[4] and he has spent virtually all of his scholarly career teaching at that institution.[5] He began at Aberdeen in 1964, and was Professor of New Testament Exegesis from 1979 until his retirement in 1999, at which time he became Honorary Research Professor. Professor Marshall has been closely connected with the Tyndale Fellowship, including chairing its committee and working with the New Testament study group, and also being involved in numerous research projects. He has published voluminously, writing important works such as his commentaries on Luke, the Johannine Epistles, Acts, 1–2 Thessalonians, 1 Peter, Philippians, and the Pastoral Epistles,[6] and publishing numerous monographs on topics such as the historical Jesus, Christology,

3. D. K. McKim, *Historical Handbook of Major Biblical Interpreters* (Downers Grove, Ill.: InterVarsity, 1998), 444–49. Some might well say that this limited scope and inclusion is a major shortcoming of this handbook.

4. As well as at Cambridge University, where he received a B.A.

5. Before coming to Aberdeen, Professor Marshall taught at Didsbury Methodist College in Bristol, and later he served in a pastorate in Darlington.

6. I. H. Marshall, *The Gospel of Luke* (New International Greek Testament Commentary; Grand Rapids: Eerdmans; Carlisle: Paternoster, 1978); *The Epistles of John* (New International Commentary on the New Testament; Grand Rapids: Eerdmans, 1978); *The Acts of the Apostles* (Tyndale New Testament Commentaries; Leicester: Inter-Varsity; Grand Rapids: Eerdmans, 1980); *1 and 2 Thessalonians* (New Century Bible; Grand Rapids: Eerdmans, 1983); *1 Peter* (IVP New Testament Commentary Series; Downers Grove, Ill.: InterVarsity; Leicester: Inter-Varsity, 1991); *The Epistle to the Philippians* (Epworth Commentaries; London:

the Last Supper, Luke-Acts, and New Testament theology.[7] He has
supervised numerous members of the next generation of New
Testament scholars, and he has contributed to the profession by
having taken up the editorship of the *Evangelical Quarterly* in
1981 from Professor Bruce, as well as editing a number of other
works.[8] Professor Marshall was presented with his Festschrift in
1994.[9] Professor Marshall also has been concerned with larger
matters of biblical interpretation. He edited the now well-known
and not-yet-replaced *New Testament Interpretation,* a volume that
had essays by a number of those associated with the second
generation of evangelical scholarship,[10] and published his valuable *Biblical Inspiration.*[11] Like F. F. Bruce before him, Howard
Marshall has been something of an enigma to some North

Epworth, 1991); (in collaboration with P. H. Towner) *A Critical and Exegetical
Commentary on the Pastoral Epistles* (International Critical Commentary; Edinburgh: Clark, 1999).

7. The following is but a sample: *Eschatology and the Parables* (London: Tyn-
dale, 1963); *Kept by the Power of God: A Study of Perseverance and Falling Away*
(London: Epworth, 1969); *The Work of Christ* (Exeter: Paternoster; Grand Rapids:
Zondervan, 1969); *Luke: Historian and Theologian* (Exeter: Paternoster; Grand
Rapids: Zondervan, 1970); *The Origins of New Testament Christology* (London:
Inter-Varsity; Downers Grove, Ill.: InterVarsity, 1976); *I Believe in the Historical
Jesus* (London: Hodder & Stoughton; Grand Rapids: Eerdmans, 1977); *Last
Supper and Lord's Supper* (Exeter: Paternoster, 1980); *Pocket Guide to Chris-
tian Beliefs* (Leicester: Inter-Varsity; Downers Grove, Ill.: InterVarsity, 1989);
Jesus the Saviour: Studies in New Testament Theology (London: SPCK; Downers
Grove, Ill.: InterVarsity, 1990); *The Acts of the Apostles* (New Testament Guides;
Sheffield: JSOT Press, 1992); (with K. P. Donfried) *The Theology of the Shorter
Pauline Letters* (Cambridge: Cambridge University Press, 1993); (with S. Travis
and I. Paul) *A Guide to the Letters and Revelation* (vol. 2 of *Exploring the New
Testament;* Downers Grove, Ill.: InterVarsity, 2002).

8. To name but a few: (with J. B. Green and S. McKnight) *Dictionary of
Jesus and the Gospels* (Downers Grove, Ill.: InterVarsity; Leicester: Inter-Varsity,
1992); *The New Bible Dictionary* (3rd ed.; Leicester: Inter-Varsity, 1996); (with D.
Peterson) *Witness to the Gospel: The Theology of the Book of Acts* (Grand Rapids:
Eerdmans, 1998); W. F. Moulton and A. S. Geden, *Concordance to the Greek New
Testament* (6th ed.; Edinburgh: Clark, 2002).

9. J. B. Green and M. Turner, eds., *Jesus of Nazareth: Lord and Christ: Essays
on the Historical Jesus and New Testament Christology* (Grand Rapids: Eerdmans;
Carlisle: Paternoster, 1994).

10. I. H. Marshall, ed., *New Testament Interpretation: Essays on Principles and
Methods* (Carlisle: Paternoster; Grand Rapids: Eerdmans, 1977).

11. I. H. Marshall, *Biblical Inspiration* (London: Hodder & Stoughton; Grand
Rapids: Eerdmans, 1982).

American evangelicals because he cannot be pigeonholed. No one can question his academic or evangelical credentials, but his conclusions have not always conformed to others' expectations. In his lectures he returns to the topic of interpretation in terms of developing an evangelical biblical theology. He is honest, gracious, autobiographical, and, perhaps most importantly, bold in his statements, born out of years of interpretative and theological experience. It is an honor for me, as a member of the so-called third generation of evangelical scholars,[12] to have been asked to respond to him in this prestigious series of lectures.

Hermeneutical Approaches to Theology

I have been interested off and on in the concept of theology as part of the larger interpretative or hermeneutical task. It is this topic that I wish to explore in my essay. It is less a direct response to Professor Marshall's three lectures—though I hope that readers will see the several direct points of correlation—than it is an attempt to set the entire enterprise of theology within a larger hermeneutical context. I cannot hope to be comprehensive in my accounting, but I wish to deal with five approaches to New Testament interpretation that have been advocated in various forms as leading from the text of Scripture to valid theology. These are (1) the historical-critical method; (2) a recent philosophical attempt based upon the philosopher Wittgenstein; (3) speech-act theory; (4) the developmental theory of Professor Marshall; and (5) my own rough attempt based upon the model provided by Paul in the New Testament. I will discuss the five approaches in order, realizing that I cannot do complete justice to any of them.

Historical-Critical Method

One of the distinguishing features of developing evangelical thought of the second half of the twentieth century—what some

12. Though not from the United Kingdom, I held a professorship there from 1994 until 2001, during which time we established a center of excellence in biblical scholarship in the institution of which I was a part and welcomed students from all over the world to study there, thus attempting to continue the tradition that Professors Bruce and Marshall established before us.

would call neoevangelicalism, as distinct from fundamental-ism—is its commitment to the use of higher-critical tools of exegesis. Some evangelical scholars might wish to differentiate between the historical-critical method and the grammatical-his-torical method.[13] The presumption appears to be that the latter is concerned with the grammar of the text and its historical context, while the former is concerned with historical matters and the kind of critical method that developed during the Enlighten-ment. I suspect that most scholars today, including evangelicals, would not wish to make such a distinction and would include grammatical study under the label of historical criticism. Rather than pursue this issue,[14] I wish to address the question of what role historical criticism can and should play in theology.

In a recent New Testament theology the author argues for a neat and tidy tripartite plan of salvation: past, present, and future.[15] The author believes that this is an apt and important way to describe the total salvation experience, especially but not exclusively in Paul. This theological position basically claims that salvation is a past, present, and future experience on the basis of the Greek tense-forms: one was saved in the past (aorist tense-form), is continuing to be saved now (present tense-form), and will be saved at the eschaton (future tense-form) (one also is saved in the past but continues to be saved in the present on the basis of the perfect tense-form). The author is concerned here with a number of crucial elements in formulating any Christian theological position. One is attention to the language of the fundamental texts of Christianity, including the actual language (Greek) of the New Testament. Another is to create some sort of valid New Testament theological framework. A further one is to

13. See, for example, R. P. Martin, "Approaches to New Testament Exegesis," in Marshall, ed., *New Testament Interpretation*, 220–51, esp. 222–23, as pointed out by Marshall in chapter 1 of the present volume.

14. For some of the issues, see I. H. Marshall, "Historical Criticism," in Mar-shall, ed., *New Testament Interpretation*, 126–37. Cf. E. Krentz, *The Historical-Critical Method* (Philadelphia: Fortress, 1975). Recent methodological discussion is revisiting the issue of historical criticism. See A. C. Thiselton, "New Testament Interpretation in Historical Perspective," in *Hearing the New Testament: Strategies for Interpretation* (ed. J. B. Green; Grand Rapids: Eerdmans, 1995), 10–36.

15. G. B. Caird, *New Testament Theology* (ed. L. D. Hurst; Oxford: Clarendon, 1994), 118–35, esp. 118–20.

make a transition from the notion of the *then* to that of the *here and now*, which the author does through the modern language of salvation experience. It is also a way to avoid falling into overly simplistic theological frameworks, such as that of conversionism—that is, what is seen as a personalization of Christianity that some are uncomfortable with and could come in the form of the question "Are you saved?" These are four crucial factors in any Christian theological framework: fidelity to the biblical witness, formulation of a contemporary theological concept, creation of a means by which this transition can move from the particularities of the original text to the contemporary world, and avoidance of overly simplistic formulations.

There is, however, a problem with this scheme: it is fundamentally wrong from a linguistic standpoint.[16] The framework is predicated upon an analysis of the Greek language that already was being seriously questioned over one hundred years ago. This conception of the Greek tense-forms is based on a temporal analysis, the kind of framework that, unfortunately, we still find all too often in first-year Greek grammar books, and that was advocated especially by German scholars until around 1880. At that time a radical shift took place in Greek language study with regard to verb structure, so that the tense-forms were seen to be concerned with *kind* of action rather than *time* of action. The result is that any analysis of tense-forms based upon a temporal framework is inherently flawed, despite what first-year Greek textbooks say. Most of those who advocate simply a time-based view of the tense-forms in Greek today have not kept up with recent investigation. The last thirty years of Greek study have revolutionized our understanding, so that the question when one sees a Greek verb tense-form is not primarily "when" but "how" is the action being depicted.[17] The result is that this neat and tidy scheme is not valid. One cannot appeal to the use of the Greek

16. The author qualifies his formulation over several places (ibid., 120–22) in what he calls a "grammatical excursion" (122), but this explanation itself is highly problematic. In effect, he maintains his original conceptual framework while admitting that there may be some loose edges.

17. Here is not the place to discuss all of the particular issues, but each of the tense-forms is problematic for the tripartite scheme being developed, including the aorist, present, and, especially, the future. The perfect tense-form is particularly problematic in this scheme. See S. E. Porter, *Verbal Aspect in the Greek of*

tense-forms to describe a tritemporal conception of salvation. Presumably, the result of this scheme is that the author does not have a simple answer according to his theological model to the question of "Are you saved?" This is not to say that he could not have formulated another scheme—for example, one could say that "I am completely saved" (aorist tense-form), "I am in progress as one who is becoming saved" (present tense-form), "I am in a saved state or condition" (perfect tense-form), and "I can expect to be saved tomorrow or some time in the future" (future tense-form)—but he does not. That scheme is mine. I think that it has both exegetical and theological validity. The answer to the question "Are you saved?" requires that the respondent know what concept of salvation the inquirer has in mind.

The failure at this particular point, however, raises a number of other questions regarding the use of the historical-critical method for the larger theological enterprise. One is the recognition that a flaw in one's historical-critical method—even if it is, as here, only one relatively small part of one's theological approach—potentially jeopardizes one's broader theological and, hence, hermeneutical enterprise. In one sense, of course, this is no different from any other academic enterprise, especially the so-called hard sciences, in which there is a necessary process of correction and even alteration of results as one proceeds.[18] However, theology perhaps is different in this regard from the scientific disciplines, as theological "test results" are not so readily available. One's current salvation is something that one may be personally certain about, but who can speak in the same way about one's ultimate destiny?

Thus, a second realization is that clearly there are limits to the historical-critical method. The method can address only historical-critical issues. These may not extend to other issues. For example, I believe that the resurrection of Jesus is something that can be analyzed using the tenets of historical study, and that the evidence from the first century is clear: a physical

the New Testament, with Reference to Tense and Mood (Studies in Biblical Greek 1; New York: Lang, 1989), 17–73, for a history of discussion, and passim for development of recent theories.

18. The classic illustration of this is found in the narrative told by T. Kuhn, *The Structure of Scientific Revolutions* (2nd ed.; Chicago: University of Chicago Press, 1970).

bodily resurrection took place, or certainly it was believed to have taken place by both the first followers of Jesus and his enemies who had him killed. However, I also can understand how some believe that the resurrection is outside the scope of modern scientific investigation because by its very nature it is a unique event that cannot be duplicated and does not conform to the scientific canon of repeatability.[19] Most historians would have to admit also that the realm of history is confined to the affairs of human beings. This excludes not only what might be more properly called the domain of science, but also what we would have to label spiritual events and, of course, God. If this is posited—that spiritual events are excluded from historical study—then we have the added difficulty of trying to differentiate between spiritual and nonspiritual events. Are the miracles of the New Testament spiritual events or not? What about the resurrection? Are they a combination of spiritual and nonspiritual events? If they are, can history deal with only the historical part, or just the consequences of the event? How do we know the difference between historical and spiritual? If these spiritual events are excluded, the result might be the exclusion of much of the New Testament from critical investigation.[20]

A further factor to consider is that the conclusions of historical-critical study might lead to conclusions that do not fit comfortably within our theological frameworks. Historic Christianity has held to particular sets of beliefs and, along with these sets of beliefs, certain other conclusions that follow from them. For example, miracles, including the physical resurrection of Jesus, are a part of that historic faith. What if the best historical-critical method were to determine that none of these could have occurred? What impact would that have upon our Christianity and Christian belief? Some might contend that this determination is impossible. Does being impossible imply that it is impossible because we have methodologically excluded such a possibility? Or do we think that the evidence is

19. I question whether this is an adequate canon, however, since many events of the past that we study as history are by their nature unrepeatable—for example, Alexander the Great's conquests. The use of analogy to other conquests, however, leaves open the use of analogy with the resurrection.

20. On historical method, see L. M. McDonald and S. E. Porter, *Early Christianity and Its Sacred Literature* (Peabody, Mass.: Hendrickson, 2000), 3–18.

so strong that it excludes it, in which case are we still open for
that evidence to be overturned? Perhaps the resurrection is not
a fair example to use. There are many other things that have
entered into discussion in post-Enlightenment criticism. These
would include, for example, questions over the words and deeds
of Jesus.[21] Historical-critical method contends that it has developed criteria by which one can determine whether Jesus actually
said or did certain things. I will put aside for the moment the
fact that scholars, using the same criteria, regularly reach quite
different conclusions regarding particular sayings or events. Instead, I wish to raise the issue of how many of these sayings or
deeds one may question as to authenticity without jeopardizing
historic Christianity. Another issue might concern pseudepigrapha in the New Testament. Most scholars contend that we have
pseudepigraphal writings in the New Testament. Many scholars
who have studied this issue also contend that pseudepigraphal
writing was not an accepted literary form of the ancient world
and implied deception and falsification.[22] Therefore, if there are
pseudepigrapha in the New Testament, they were introduced
through some deceptive or falsified means. What implications
are there for understanding the New Testament and creating a
theology based upon texts that at best are of unknown authorship and at worst were written with bad intentions? Or, as some
have even suggested, do we open up our canon for further ad-
ditions, or purge it of those works that are now seen not to be
justifiable historically as authentic? Or, are there limits to the
work that we do as evangelical scholars? As Professor Marshall
says in his first lecture, "As Christian scholars who adhere to
the evangelical faith, we are committed *to the academic study
of Scripture* within a confessional framework, and therefore we
must consider how this situation both liberates and constrains
us as we carry out this task." This is not a fashionable thing to
say in some circles, since it threatens to circumvent the historical-critical process when things get too tough (and has done so

21. For a trenchant critique of such an enterprise, see L. T. Johnson, *The Real
Jesus: The Misguided Quest for the Historical Jesus and the Truth of the Traditional
Gospels* (San Francisco: HarperSanFrancisco, 1996).

22. See L. R. Donelson, *Pseudepigraphy and Ethical Argument in the Pastoral
Epistles* (Hermeneutische Untersuchungen zur Theologie 22; Tübingen: Mohr,
1986), 11.

in some circles). On the other hand, the appeal to the inevitable fact that every interpreter is positioned and situated historically, theologically, ideologically, and so forth, runs directly contrary to the historical method itself and loses ground for an objective appeal.[23] This surely accounts for why so many scholars disagree over whether Jesus said this or that or did something else, and whether Paul wrote certain letters. Perhaps we should simply face the inevitable, that there are no completely objective interpreters and that interpretation is to a large extent based upon presupposition as well as predisposition. In that sense, theology precedes exegesis, and hermeneutics dictates criticism.

The last factor to consider is that there has been no method developed by historical criticism to bridge Lessing's "ditch." Lessing observed that there is no historical method by which the "accidental truths of history [i.e., the ephemeral events that make up history] can . . . become the proof of necessary truths of reason."[24] Some of the other methods that I will examine below attempt to make such a leap (some would call it a leap of faith, no doubt), but so far the historical method has not found a way to do so. This makes philosophical sense in that the events of history, as one-off situated occurrences, contain no interpretation in and of themselves, but simply are events. One might well observe that many of the events of the New Testament do in fact contain such interpretation (e.g., Paul's interpretation of the sacrificial death of Jesus). However, these interpretations themselves, so the logic goes, are situated and certainly are not the only interpretations, either then or now.

What are we to conclude regarding the historical-critical method? The exaltation of the historical-critical method, in nineteenth- and especially twentieth-century scholarship, contained much optimism. However, its results clearly are circumscribed and limited. The use of the method has helped us to understand more about some of the events that transpired thousands of

23. This is where the double edge of postmodernism cuts both ways. It allows all voices at the table but also makes it impossible to say which voice or voices should be heard.

24. G. E. Lessing, "On the Proof of the Spirit and of Power," in *Lessing's Theological Writings* (ed. H. Chadwick; London: Black, 1956), 56; cited in A. C. Thiselton, *The Two Horizons: New Testament Hermeneutics and Philosophical Description* (Grand Rapids: Eerdmans, 1980), 64, where there is critical discussion.

years ago. For example, the use of some of the recently published
Qumran documents has substantiated much of the traditional
portrait of Jesus as a messianic figure and what he meant when
he uttered particular statements. This study verges on apolo-
getics as much as it does historical criticism. However, I am
unconvinced that all of these proposed results are necessarily
correct, nor am I sure that New Testament studies has really
gained much when it ends up doubting more than it affirms
regarding the historical Jesus. The scholarly guild may think
that it knows more, but whether the person in the pew is ben-
efited by such knowledge (if it is knowledge) is doubtful. Thus,
despite whatever benefits it may have, historical criticism is
not, to my mind, the means by which we best do theology, nor
is it the hermeneutical key to understanding Scripture in a
contemporary context.

Wittgenstein's Classes of Utterances

I have long been interested in finding a means by which one
can bridge Lessing's ditch. One of the weaknesses of the historical-critical method, as noted above, is that it does not have
a means of moving from the historical particularity of then to
generalizations or universals that pertain now, or, to put it in a
distinctly theological context, from what God said then to what
God says now. History is full of attempts to bridge this gap. A
number of years ago I tackled what I then called the ethical issue
of Gal. 3:28–29 by invoking a scheme by Anthony Thiselton that
appealed to three different classes of utterances as described by
the philosopher Ludwig Wittgenstein.[25] Thiselton differentiated
three classes of utterances in Wittgenstein's thought that he saw
as having potential for labeling and hence describing the function of natural language statements, such as might be found in

25. S. E. Porter, "Wittgenstein's Classes of Utterances and Pauline Ethical
Texts," *Journal of the Evangelical Theological Society* 32 (1989): 85–97; reprinted
with modifications as "Wittgenstein's Classes of Utterances and Pauline Ethical
Texts: A Study of Galatians 3:28–29 in Context," in S. E. Porter, *Studies in the
Greek New Testament: Theory and Practice* (Studies in Biblical Greek 6; New York:
Lang, 1996), 239–54 (which I cite in this essay, which draws upon Thiselton's
examples). See the discussion of Wittgenstein in Thiselton, *The Two Horizons*,
357–407.

Scripture. The notion was that if this classificatory scheme was operative, appropriate labeling would define how a statement made then would have relevance now.

The three categories of utterance that Thiselton designated and that I utilized can be outlined as follows.

First-class utterance. A first-class utterance is a neutral or universal grammatical utterance, similar to the analytical or a priori utterances of logical positivism, and hence not culturally relative.[26] An example is Rom. 11:6: "If it is by grace, then it is no longer by works; if it were, grace would no longer be grace." In other words, grace and works are mutually exclusive. Another example is Rom. 4:4: "When one works, wages are not credited as a gift, but as an obligation." A third example is Rom. 13:10: "Love does no harm to its neighbor."

Second-class utterance. A second-class utterance is the expression of the attitude of a particular cultural or religious tradition, which constitutes the "scaffolding" around which our thoughts are organized.[27] An example is Rom. 3:4–6, where Paul raises the question of whether God is unjust in bringing anger upon humans, since if he were, he could not judge the world. Another example is Rom. 9:14–24, which relies upon a human convention that says that God's verdicts cannot be questioned by guilty people.

Third-class utterance. A third-class utterance is a hypothetical statement that challenges the accepted means of thinking and results in a new and provocative view of the established structures of thought as found in second-class utterances.[28] An example is Rom. 2:28–29: "A person is not a Jew who is only one outwardly, nor is circumcision merely outward and physical. No, a person is a Jew who is one inwardly; and circumcision is circumcision of the heart."

Such a set of classifications contains at least the potential for cutting a number of Gordian knots. If we were able to classify each utterance of the New Testament, we could establish a clear difference between culturally bound statements (second-class

26. See also A. J. Ayer, *Language, Truth, and Logic* (2nd ed.; New York: Dover, 1952), 84, and passim.

27. Thiselton, *The Two Horizons*, 392, citing L. Wittgenstein, *On Certainty* (Oxford: Blackwell, 1969), §211.

28. See Thiselton, *The Two Horizons*, 401–2.

utterances) and timeless ones (first-class utterances), or between new ways of viewing a state of affairs (third-class utterances) and the old ones. In other words, we would be able finally to show (so one might hope) that all of the passages about restricting women's roles in ministry are nothing more than second-class utterances, and the debate over women in ministry would be over. Or we would be able to classify those passages on homosexuality and show once and for all that they are timeless first-class utterances as much to be obeyed today as yesterday, and a number of denominations could relax. Unfortunately, my further investigation showed that such classification is flawed in many regards, in terms of both theory and application.

The inherent flaws in the method can be enumerated briefly.[29] The first criticism is that this scheme—especially the first-class utterances—is vulnerable to the standard criticism of logical positivism: the verifiability principle itself is unverified.[30] In other words, to invoke the positive criterion of self-evident or tautological truths requires an intuitive leap that is not substantiated either by self-evident truths or empiricism. A second criticism follows: self-evident or tautological truths are a matter of opinion, or, to put it otherwise, are themselves culturally conditioned. What is self-evident or tautological to one person may well be debatable to another. For example, the statement "God is love" is not a self-evident statement to logical positivists (many significant logical positivists questioned the existence of God), but it is self-evident to many Christians, no matter what else they may think about God.[31] A third criticism is that the link between first-class utterances and the empirical world is tenuous. For example, roundness is part of what it means to be a circle, but only in certain geometric worlds. The shortest distance between two points is not necessarily a straight line in

29. For more detailed criticism, see Porter, "Classes of Utterances," 243–49.

30. See W. T. Jones, *The Twentieth Century to Wittgenstein and Sartre* (vol. 5 of *A History of Western Philosophy;* 2nd ed.; New York: Harcourt Brace Jovanovich, 1975), esp. 220–22, 245–48.

31. In fact, Clark Pinnock, my colleague at McMaster Divinity College, has helped to construct an entire theology around this notion. See, for example, C. H. Pinnock, *Most Moved Mover: A Theology of God's Openness* (Carlisle: Paternoster; Grand Rapids: Baker, 2001), esp. 113–51 in a chapter entitled "The Metaphysics of Love."

"donut geometry" (a geometry in which the donut, rather than the plane, is fundamental). A fourth criticism is that, especially concerning second-class utterances, it is surprising that so much of the agreed framework of culture has been so recently overthrown. It is as if, to use Wittgenstein's terminology, these utterances are simply part of a language game in which the language use is confined to that particular language game and does not reach outside itself to something other. This would make the resulting theology merely contextual—no more than contextual, without being transcendent. A fifth criticism is that distinguishing between second- and third-class utterances requires more contextual knowledge than we may possess. If so, then there is the further question of what relationship a third-class utterance has to reality, since it is purported to be a picture of a new way of viewing things. It is hard to imagine a picture of something new that does not make significant use of the old. In this case, we are simply back to the second-class utterance.

There are two further, encompassing criticisms of a particular sort that must also be registered. The first is that virtually every one of the biblical examples that Thiselton introduces in his elucidation of Wittgenstein's notions can be, and probably has been in some way, questioned. In my article, among other examples, I analyzed in more detail the use that Richard Longenecker makes of Gal. 3:28–29 in his book on social ethics.[32] I discovered that despite Longenecker's desire to use this New Testament passage as the basis of social ethics, there are problems with such use, even in his own exposition. He seems to treat it as a first-class utterance, but then he describes it in terms of a third-class utterance as setting forth a new relationship, and he concludes by saying that it may already have been widely used as a baptismal liturgy of the early church, a second-class utterance. In other words, even so ostensibly clear a statement as is found in Gal. 3:28–29 is problematic within even a single treatment. The second broader criticism is that this kind of Wittgensteinian scheme was never intended to bridge the gap from what is being described to what should be—that

32. R. N. Longenecker, *New Testament Social Ethics for Today* (Grand Rapids: Eerdmans, 1984), esp. 27, 30, 31–33, 34, but also throughout. Longenecker is discussed in more detail in Porter, "Classes of Utterances," 250.

is, between the historical situation that elicited the text and the world in which it is to be applied or lived.[33] And, indeed, from what I have discovered, it cannot.

Speech–Act Theory

Having examined a more traditional historical-based model, and one dependent upon a more abstract philosophical model,[34] I now turn to a model of hermeneutics that recently has come into its own. Much recent work has been done in both biblical and theological studies on speech-act theory as a way forward in hermeneutics and theology. Speech-act theory is a set of pragmatically based principles that were developed at the edge of philosophy and linguistics. The major assumption is that language is not so much concerned with *saying* as with *doing*.[35] That is, the use of language is in fact a way of accomplishing things. As a result, a vigorous debate has been conducted among a number of philosopher-linguists over language and what it can and cannot do. The major thought on this topic grows from the work of the so-called ordinary language philosophers, the most well known being J. L. Austin and John Searle.[36] Their thought

33. See L. Wittgenstein, *Tractatus Logico-Philosophicus* (1921; trans. D. F. Pears and B. F. McGuiness; London: Routledge & Kegan Paul, 1961), 71 §6.42.

34. That model draws more upon the earlier Wittgenstein, such as is found in *Tractatus Logico-Philosophicus*. The later Wittgenstein tended toward ordinary language philosophy, such as is found in his *Philosophical Investigations* (trans. G. E. M. Anscombe; 2nd ed.; Oxford: Blackwell, 1958).

35. S. C. Levinson, *Pragmatics* (Cambridge: Cambridge University Press, 1983), 228.

36. J. L. Austin, *How to Do Things with Words* (Oxford: Clarendon, 1962); J. R. Searle, *Speech Acts: An Essay in the Philosophy of Language* (Cambridge: Cambridge University Press, 1969); idem, *Expression and Meaning: Studies in the Theory of Speech Acts* (Cambridge: Cambridge University Press, 1979). See also C. E. Caton, ed., *Philosophy and Ordinary Language* (Urbana: University of Illinois Press, 1963). Besides ordinary language philosophy (and theologians noted below), speech-act theory has developed in at least three areas of potential relevance for biblical scholars and theologians: the linguistic area of pragmatics (e.g., Levinson, *Pragmatics*, 226–83; F. H. van Eemeren and R. Grootendorst, *Speech Acts in Argumentative Discussions: A Theoretical Model for the Analysis of Discussions Directed towards Solving Conflicts of Opinion* [Dordrecht: Foris, 1984]; J. L. Mey, *Pragmatics: An Introduction* [Oxford: Blackwell, 1993], 109–29), theoretical linguistics (e.g., J. M. Sadock, *Toward a Linguistic Theory of Speech*

has been taken up by a number of biblical scholars and theologians and applied to the kinds of historical, textual, literary, and theological issues that we face. Two of the best known among these are Anthony Thiselton and Kevin Vanhoozer.[37]

In recent work the precepts of speech-act theory have been drawn (even if slowly and in a halting way) into not only New Testament studies, as an attempt to come to terms with textual and authorial intention, but also broader hermeneutical issues, including theology. Since Austin, speech-act theorists posit that language can be used to perform three different kinds of acts.[38]

Acts [New York: Academic Press, 1974]; J. J. Katz, *Propositional Structure and Illocutionary Force: A Study of the Contribution of Sentence Meaning to Speech Acts* [Cambridge: Harvard University Press, 1980]), and literary theory (e.g., M. L. Pratt, *Toward a Speech Act Theory of Literary Discourse* [Bloomington: Indiana University Press, 1977]; S. Petrey, *Speech Acts and Literary Theory* [New York: Routledge, 1990]).

37. Among many works, see A. C. Thiselton, *New Horizons in Hermeneutics: The Theory and Practice of Transforming Biblical Reading* (Grand Rapids: Zondervan, 1992); idem, "Thirty Years of Hermeneutics: Retrospect and Prospects," in *The Interpretation of the Bible: The International Symposium in Slovenia* (ed. J. Krassovec; Journal for the Study of the Old Testament: Supplement Series 289; Sheffield: Sheffield Academic Press, 1998), 1559–74; idem, "Communicative Action and Promise in Interdisciplinary, Biblical, and Theological Hermeneutics," in R. Lundin, C. Walhout, and A. C. Thiselton, *The Promise of Hermeneutics* (Grand Rapids: Eerdmans, 1999), 133–239 (with Thiselton's bibliography [144 n. 30]); K. J. Vanhoozer, *Is There a Meaning in This Text? The Bible, the Reader, and the Morality of Literary Knowledge* (Grand Rapids: Zondervan, 1998); idem, "From Speech Acts to Scripture Acts: The Covenant of Discourse and the Discourse of Covenant," in *After Pentecost: Language and Biblical Interpretation* (ed. C. Bartholomew, C. Greene, and K. Möller; Carlisle: Paternoster, 2001), 1–49. I am relying mostly upon Vanhoozer's recent monograph. Many of the relevant issues are raised, discussed, and summarized in R. S. Briggs, *Words in Action: Speech Act Theory and Biblical Interpretation* (Edinburgh: Clark, 2001); Briggs has bibliography for the aforementioned writers and others. For examples of those who have applied speech-act theory to biblical interpretation, see J. Botha, *Jesus and the Samaritan Woman: A Speech Act Reading of John 4:1–42* (Novum Testamentum Supplements 65; Leiden: Brill, 1991); D. Neufeld, *Reconceiving Texts as Speech Acts: An Analysis of I John* (Biblical Interpretation Series 7; Leiden: Brill, 1994); A. C. Thiselton, *The First Epistle to the Corinthians* (New International Greek Testament Commentary; Grand Rapids: Eerdmans; Carlisle: Paternoster, 2000).

38. See Vanhoozer, *Is There a Meaning?* 209, and passim; Thiselton, "Thirty Years of Hermeneutics," 1562; cf. Levinson, *Pragmatics*, 236. This tripartite schema of performative language has subsequently been refined as the theory has developed, but it remains the essential set of distinctions.

First, the locutionary act is what someone does in speaking or writing a word, as in simply uttering "good-bye," for instance. Second, the illocutionary act is what someone does in saying or writing something, such as making a statement, offering, promising, in accordance with the conventional or institutional force that is associated with the act.[39] Third, the perlocutionary act is what is brought about or caused by saying or writing something, and what is particular to the circumstances in which this utterance is made. For example,[40] the locutionary act of my saying "I now bestow upon you, Dr. Craig Evans, the Payzant Chair in New Testament" has the illocutionary force of actually bestowing this chair upon him only if there are felicitous conditions for doing so, such as my being the principal of Acadia Divinity College, and there being a chair with this name, and there being an occasion for such a bestowal. If all those conditions exist (as they did on October 17, 2002), then the perlocutionary act of bestowing that chair has taken place. Similarly, if someone says "I do" one time too many, that person may not be married twice, but rather committing the crime of polygamy (depending, of course, upon the conventions and laws in force).

The invocation of language as action has been used by both Thiselton and especially Vanhoozer (and now Briggs) as an attempt to rescue current theological interpretation from the slippery slope of postmodernism, especially as it is found in deconstructionism. For this, they are no doubt to be commended. As concomitants to this program, Vanhoozer in particular resurrects and revives several other notions along the way. These include the stability and presence of the author in terms of intentionality. They wish to move away from a psychological intentionality, the kind of thing attacked by Wimsatt and Beardsley as the intentional fallacy,[41] to a kind of communicative intention that stands behind and motivates locutionary acts and invests them with illocutionary force. Vanhoozer uses this platform to

39. See Briggs, *Words in Action*, 51.

40. I use this example because I gave the earlier form of this lecture at Acadia Divinity College in conjunction with participating in the installation of Craig Evans in the Payzant Chair on October 17, 2002.

41. W. K. Wimsatt and M. Beardsley, "The Intentional Fallacy," in *The Verbal Icon: Studies in the Meaning of Poetry* (Lexington: University of Kentucky Press, 1954), 3–18. See Vanhoozer, *Is There a Meaning?* 82–85.

establish what he calls his "critical hermeneutical realism,"[42] in which there is "enacted communicative intention" in the text and accessible to readers.[43] The author standing behind every communicative act provides the basis for creating an ethics of interpretation, in which it is therefore possible to validate and invalidate readings. Vanhoozer also utilizes a form of E. D. Hirsch's distinction between meaning and significance to differentiate between what the illocutionary force of an utterance may have been and all sorts of other meanings and things that have been done with it since, the kinds of things that may be categorized under the rubric of perlocutionary force.[44] As a last major category for interpretation, Vanhoozer develops a theory of genre—more specifically, generic illocutions—as a guide to these intentions.[45]

Vanhoozer's recent work has garnered much attention in evangelical theological circles. His work has shown that it is possible to argue rigorously (and at length) for a number of fundamental notions, even some that some people believe to have already passed on. Thus, Vanhoozer provides a convincing case for a focused definition of intentionality in the midst of a theological environment that seems to have wanted to abandon such a concept. However, I wonder if all of the effort was well directed. My criticisms of speech-act theory as a hermeneutical platform for theological construct building are focused on two areas. One is in terms of Vanhoozer's own theory, and the other is in terms of speech-act theory itself.

In terms of Vanhoozer's own theory, there is much to commend his knowledge of the sources, but there are a surprising number of major problems. One is his theory of genre. Theories of genre are notoriously difficult to defend, since most theories—and Vanhoozer's must fall into this category—require a

42. Vanhoozer, *Is There a Meaning?* 320. I do not see where Vanhoozer says where he gets the notion of critical hermeneutical realism. An earlier work concerned with similar issues is B. F. Meyer, *Critical Realism and the New Testament* (Allison Park, Pa.: Pickwick, 1989).

43. Vanhoozer, *Is There a Meaning?* 320.

44. Ibid., 374–76, 427–29. See E. D. Hirsch, *Validity in Interpretation* (New Haven: Yale University Press, 1967); idem, "Meaning and Significance Reinterpreted," *Critical Inquiry* 11 (1984): 202–24.

45. Vanhoozer, *Is There a Meaning?* 340–42.

near ontological status to be of value for their interpretative program. In other words, there must be almost a Platonic type of genre in order to have it carry the interpretative weight that Vanhoozer attempts to put onto it. To my mind, Vanhoozer does not address the more fundamental issue of the cultural dependence and contextualization of genres. We may think that we now have a clear notion of what a novel or a Gospel entails as a genre, but that is seen in terms of the other genres that we may have available. How such a category (if it is even pertinent at all, such as novel) may have functioned in the ancient world is another matter. Vanhoozer goes further and seems to posit that the Gospels may be unique generically,[46] but I am not sure that that helps his case, since it is unclear where a new genre would come from and how it would be understood, and it would seem to fight against the kind of certainty in interpretation that he seeks by using a static notion of genre.

A further question arises with Vanhoozer's use of the speech-act format, in which he seems to imply that the illocutionary acts themselves have some kind of ontological status. At one point he implies that perhaps the illocutionary act of marrying follows a divinely ordered speech act, what amounts to a sacramental view of language.[47] This seems to run contrary to the kind of thinking that speech-act theory entails, but shifts much of what Vanhoozer is saying to an ontological or metaphysical debate. This is confirmed in the sense that he places a high priority upon an incarnational and Trinitarian theology.[48] I have no problem with this theological stance, except that this reflects a completely different starting point for his discussion than beginning with ordinary language philosophy—a position that threatens to stage an end run around some of the difficult issues of such philosophy.

Lastly, there is the issue of how one uses the notion of authorial intention. Vanhoozer does not actually do much extended interpretation of texts and show how he would utilize these in-

46. Ibid., 340, where Vanhoozer says that each literary kind, including Gospel, has its own distinctive features.

47. Ibid., 213–14. I may share Vanhoozer's view of marriage, but I doubt that this view comes from one's use of speech-act theory.

48. Ibid., 456, and passim.

terpretations in construction of a theology. In the way his system is constructed, I find it difficult to know how it is that he would adjudicate a dispute over a crucial or contentious issue using his method. The fact that opposing sides would have differences of opinion might elicit the response that at least we were appealing to common ground—that is, those who hold to such things as authorial intention, that texts have meaning, and the like. However, my suspicion is that for the most part Vanhoozer's conversation was with these people anyway, so I am not sure what has been gained.

More perplexing perhaps is Vanhoozer's and others' recent use of speech-act theory in light of developments in the linguistic field of pragmatics. Speech-act theory grew out of ordinary language philosophy. Note that it is ordinary language *philosophy*, not ordinary language *linguistics*. There is a difference. Speech-act theory developed out of distinction from truth-conditional semantics and out of logical positivism.[49] This does not mean that ordinary language philosophy is actually attuned to studying the real use of language in context, but only that it is better at doing so than forms of symbolic logic. What was gained by abandoning the kind of logical positivist agenda may have been sacrificed, so far as Vanhoozer and others are concerned, by the loss of a truth-based semantic base. If speech-act theory contends that uses of language are not reducible to matters of truth and falsity, but merely communicative intention or action, then I am not sure what role they may be said to play within a theological framework such as the one that Vanhoozer is constructing.[50]

A second problem is that discussion of speech acts does not address what might be called special uses of sentences, in which they do not carry the kind of full force that they would in everyday conversation. In other words, speech-act theory has not created a poetics of language, suitable for discussion of literary forms, such as novel, drama, and poetry.[51] The relation, therefore, of speech-act theory to the writings of the

49. See Levinson, *Pragmatics*, 227.
50. Ibid., 243–46. I realize that Vanhoozer wishes to ground the discussion in a larger theological framework, but that exists independently of speech-act theory.
51. Ibid., 228.

Bible is unclear. This perhaps accounts for the fact that so little actual analysis of Scripture has taken place using this model. Vanhoozer wants to use speech-act theory inclusively in his hermeneutical framework, but it appears that there was never any intention to do such (this raises questions in itself regarding the notion of intentionality, if Vanhoozer thinks that he can use the theory in ways that it was never intended). Speech-act analysis is highly dependent upon the felicitous conditions that lead to locutions.[52] In other words, one needs already to know the *context* in which particular utterances are made. Obviously, literary contexts are artificial and do not carry that kind of reality with them. In terms of an ancient context, there is not only the issue of what kind of written text one is dealing with (e.g., Jonah: is it historical narrative or fiction?), but also the even more pressing issue of having suitable context to be able to appreciate the illocutionary and hence perlocutionary force of a speech act.

The last point to note is that twenty years ago in linguistic circles there was already a move away from speech-act theory.[53] It was already being recognized that speech-act theory had a number of internal difficulties that made it unusable as a workable pragmatic model. For example, Levinson has noted that most speech-act analysis is concerned with categorizing speech acts, which is done either arbitrarily (so much for objective interpretation or critical realism) or on the basis of function or result (perlocutionary force), something virtually impossible to judge for the biblical text.[54] Even in contemporary language use the contextual issues have proved too complex for such a theory. As a result, various forms of discourse analysis have taken the place of speech-act theory and have proved much more profitable; many detailed and sustained analyses of texts have been made.[55] I am not aware of any discourse analytic theory of hermeneutics and theology, however. Perhaps one merits development.

52. Ibid., 246–63.
53. Ibid., 278–83.
54. Ibid., 278.
55. Discourse analysis has many forms, but some of the most productive of these have close links to functional linguistics, which itself is linked to ordinary or natural language linguistics.

The Developmental Theory of I. Howard Marshall

Professor Marshall presents a developmental theory that he has formulated. In his three lectures he shows how it is that an experienced exegete wrestles with major issues that are faced in terms of developing a theology. As he outlines in his first lecture, his method of moving from general hermeneutical issues to exegesis to exposition or application has much merit to it. He also surveys other methods that have entered the arena, without necessarily pushing out older interpretative methods. Evangelical scholarship faces the same issues. In fact, he notes that in some areas evangelicals have done some of the most significant work, both in hermeneutics and especially in exegesis. It is in the area of exposition or application that he begins to register his valid complaints.

He takes up this issue more fully in his second lecture, where he outlines various approaches to ethics, ecclesiology, and theology. He chooses to concentrate on issues of doctrine, where he cites six examples—open theism, penal substitution, the nature of hell, the penalty for those who have not heard the gospel, ecumenism with regard to episcopal churches, and the question of a sacramental view of the Lord's Supper—that display development in Christian doctrine beyond Scripture's express comments. He notes that the concerns of liberalism with weighing Scripture according to contemporary standards have some merit in the modern world. Before he attempts to resolve this issue, he notes three types of development that he sees within Scripture itself. These occur in the use of the Old Testament (e.g., understanding of God), the teaching of Jesus (e.g., in John's Gospel), and the apostolic teaching (e.g., the Pastoral Epistles).[56] Thus, the New Testament itself bears witness to theological development.

It is this model of development that he explicates in his third lecture. In that lecture he uses the interpretation of the book of Leviticus in the New Testament as the means of discerning principles by which we can interpret the New Testament for our contemporary use. These include that the old covenant is

56. Those who do not accept the pseudepigraphal nature of the Pastoral Epistles probably will find this last example less convincing. Professor Marshall calls his view "allonymity" (see Marshall, *Pastoral Epistles*, 57–92, where he attempts to address the issue of deception in pseudonymity).

distinguished from the new covenant; sacrifices point to Jesus' death; ethical principles can be drawn even if rituals are not maintained; and Scripture is seen to apply to all of those in the new covenant, Jews and Gentiles alike. He also looks at Jesus' teaching in light of this developmental model, and he sees that the Christology depicted is elementary; a sacrificial understanding of Jesus' own death is not developed; the Holy Spirit is not an understandable doctrine; Easter significantly changes Jesus' relation to his followers; Jesus' own teaching reflects a period of transition and must be seen in light of his death and resurrection; and Jesus' imagery accommodates to the understanding of his contemporary hearers. Thus, he proposes that there are four trends in the early church that provide a model for contemporary interpretation: the identification of a theological error that needs to be addressed, appeal to teaching already established, appeal to insight already nurtured by the Spirit, and development of appropriate responses to address the problem in fresh ways.

This short summary is not meant to substitute for a careful reading of Professor Marshall's essays. Far from it, since his broad conclusions regarding how to read the Old Testament in light of Jesus, his view of how to understand Jesus' teaching, and his approach to understanding other apostolic teaching display a meritorious grappling with issues such as doctrinal development throughout the Bible, the importance of treating the whole of the scriptural witness, seeing continuity from the Old Testament to the New Testament, and providing a principled means of doing so. However, my comments elsewhere in this essay lead me to believe that there will be some who wish to raise further questions. One of the major questions probably will be, How do we know the difference between cultural baggage and contemporary inconvenience? At one point, in addressing the particularly harsh language of divine retribution and punishment found in the parables of Jesus, Professor Marshall says, "There would be universal agreement among civilized people that no human being should perpetrate horrors of the kind described in the parabolic imagery." Similarly, he finds it "incredible that God should so act," which alerts him to the fact that imagery in the Bible, such as in the parables, belongs to a specific time of the past. This might well be seen to beg the very question that we are trying to answer, however, which is not just what civilized people, but rather what Christians of today, should think about such actions. The statement that it is incredible that God should so act raises questions about the nature of God within such a developmental hypothesis, and whether this kind of developmental consistency can be maintained. Further questions inevitably will be raised concerning what it means that Scripture is seen as incomplete; how it is that the whole of Scripture helps understanding if the particular parts are problematic; and, finally, how one is to test and evaluate one's contemporary understandings against a scriptural norm that itself is seen as undeveloped and shifting. Nevertheless, Professor Marshall clearly has raised the right kinds of questions and proposed some sensible answers to the quest for developing an evangelical hermeneutic.

The Pauline Model and Translational Theory

I now have arrived at that place in this essay, the final point of my five-point outline, where I am supposed to pull a hermeneutical rabbit out of the exegetical hat (or is it an exegetical rabbit out of the hermeneutical hat?) and wow my audience with my ability to make even the most complex issues come clear. As the reader can well imagine, after the discussion that I have just offered, things aren't quite that simple. In fact, I hope that through the course of reading Professor Marshall's lectures, and perhaps through what little I have added, readers can appreciate that the move from the original text of Scripture, with all of its time-bound character, to theological truths for life today is one of the most demanding intellectual tasks imaginable. It is Lessing's ditch, still to be traversed. Yet it is an intellectual and theological necessity, especially for those of us who take Scripture and the Christian life seriously. It is in fact virtually identical to the kind of intellectual task confronted by preachers and teachers of the Word every time they open the Bible to read, "Thus saith the Lord." Anyone who proclaims how easy it is to do this is probably prevaricating, or is very bad at the task, or is so very experienced at it as to have forgotten the intellectual and spiritual task that it is.

In thinking through what my contribution to this discussion with Professor Marshall might be, I wish to bring us back to the

greatest interpreter of the truths of Christianity in the New Testament, the apostle Paul (who arguably is also the greatest interpreter of the last two millennia). I know that some will counter that
the Gospel writers were interpreters of the Christ event, and yes,
that is true (although others dispute that formulation); but what
I mean is that in terms of someone taking the data of Christianity
and applying them in what we would see as a contemporary theological framework, the model has to be Paul. Rather than present-
ing a full-blown hermeneutical method that moves from the text
of Scripture to principlized timeless theological truths, I wish to
explore the implications of what Paul models for us in his letters
in the New Testament. So, what characteristics did Paul display
in his taking the events of early Christianity and formulating them
into the basis of what it meant to be a follower of Christ?

I suggest, first, that Paul held a number of beliefs that provided
the matrix by which he viewed all of the other data, and, second,
that the notion of translation provides a means of interpreting
the text that we can utilize today. Briefly, I suggest that three
fundamental beliefs governed Paul's thinking.[57] The first and
foremost of these was the theological center of his thought,
God.[58] Paul never doubts, questions, or wavers in his belief that
God not only exists but also is active in the world, and was especially active in the life and death of Jesus Christ. He assumes that
the God of the Old Testament, who made his abiding covenant
with Abraham (Rom. 4:3), is the same God who is at work in the
world to create and redeem a new people of God for his calling.
It is this God who demonstrates his love for humans by creating
the means for their redemption (Rom. 8:29–30).[59]

The second belief is the christological center of his thought.
Jesus Christ as Lord and Savior[60] (there are subversive political

57. I explore these in more detail in McDonald and Porter, *Early Christianity*,
352–57.

58. A good introduction to some of these issues is N. Richardson, *Paul's
Language about God* (Journal for the Study of the New Testament: Supplement
Series 99; Sheffield: Sheffield Academic Press, 1994).

59. One could also cite proto-Trinitarian texts in Paul's writings as evidence
of his theological belief being central to his beliefs about the Christian life. See,
for example, Rom. 1:1–7; 2 Cor. 13:13.

60. I note the similarity to the title of Professor Marshall's *Jesus the Saviour:
Studies in New Testament Theology*.

tones to what he says here)[61] and his death and resurrection stand at the heart of all else that Paul believed. This can be seen in so many ways that I hesitate to begin enumerating them. One is in terms of the confessional and creedal passages that Paul uses, whether these came from Paul himself or were earlier statements used within the Christian community.[62] Virtually every one of them has affirmation of the death and resurrection of Jesus Christ as essential to its formulation. Here I am thinking of, for example, Rom. 1:3–4; 1 Cor. 15; Phil. 2:6–11; Col. 1:15–20. And the notion of the death and resurrection of Jesus Christ runs throughout Paul's letters in other ways as well. This constitutes the heart of what Paul wants to say about Jesus and consequently what it means to be a Christian—one in some way participates in the power of that death and resurrection. In this sense, there is clearly a theological core to Paul's belief. It is much larger than this, I think, but it is at least this. As one moves out from the center, it probably is harder to pin down some issues versus others (e.g., eschatology), but that does not mean that they were unimportant to him or that he did not believe certain things about them, but only that it is more difficult for us to define them.

The third belief, which follows from this, is that Paul held that Christians are those who follow Jesus Christ. Of course, that seems to state the obvious, but judging from what I see around me, I think that it is far from self-evident. Paul believed that one should be able to see Christ in the life of the believer. Paul modeled this by talking of himself as an imitator of Christ and as one to be emulated by believers (1 Cor. 4:16; 11:1; Eph. 5:1; 1 Thess. 1:6; 2 Thess. 3:7, 9). His life bore this out in terms of the sacrifice and hardship that he endured for the sake of

61. I believe that the language that Paul uses, especially in places such as the opening of the book of Romans (1:1–17), although quite possibly elsewhere also, reflects an anti-imperial theology in which Jesus, not Caesar, is Lord (God) and Savior. The direct correlations of the language—good news, Son of God, Lord, God as Father, grace, salvation—are striking. A sample of imperial texts is found in V. Ehrenberg and A. H. M. Jones, *Documents Illustrating the Reigns of Augustus and Tiberius* (2nd ed.; Oxford: Clarendon, 1955), 81–97.

62. I realize that many claim that these statements predate Paul, but I do not wish to forestall debate on this point. I am inclined to believe that at least some of them may well have originated with Paul, even if not on the occasion of the writing of the individual letter.

the gospel (2 Cor. 11:23–27). It is significant that there is much discussion over whether Phil. 2:6–11 is meant to be doctrinal or ethical in nature.[63] Perhaps this is a false dichotomy, and instead it should be both; ethics and theology are linked together. In any case, for Paul, Christianity is lived Christianity, not static Christianity. This is reflected in the Pauline letter form, where praxis (paraenesis) follows on from theology.[64]

Paul also did a fair bit of modeling for us of how to understand and interpret Scripture in light of these beliefs (I could cite more, of course). The book of Romans is a case in point. Paul had an uncanny ability to move through and with the text that exemplifies to us how to do our biblically based theology. His hermeneutical principles were complex, but a couple of them are worth noting briefly here. One is that he is able to differentiate between what was essential and what was contingent in the text. He can cite specific examples from the Old Testament without their specificity holding back the meaning of the text for his contemporary situation. One thinks, for example, of how Paul uses the Old Testament, with its statements addressed to the people of Israel, to describe his belief in the future role of Israel in conjunction with the Christian church (Rom. 9–11). Another is that Paul can pay attention to each letter without becoming overly literalistic. This is not an easy task, but it is one that many of us could learn from. An example is his distinction in Gal. 3:16 between "seed" and "seeds," not to make a pedantic point but to rightly interpret the Old Testament narrative through the eyes of his Christology. Thus, to form a complete theology as Christians, it appears that we must read the Old Testament in terms of the New Testament, just as Paul and the other New Testament writers read it in light of their christological understandings. So far, Professor Marshall and I probably would agree on most of these issues. What about the understanding of the New Testa-

---

63. See S. Fowl, *The Story of Christ in the Ethics of Paul: An Analysis of the Function of the Hymnic Material in the Pauline Corpus* (Journal for the Study of the New Testament: Supplement Series 36; Sheffield: JSOT Press, 1990), 77–101.

64. On the letter form, see McDonald and Porter, *Early Christianity*, 380–86. Those who believe that Paul is concerned only with theology (and that "works" are shunned at all levels) should consider further the importance of the Pauline letter form and what the paraenetic sections contain.

ment, where we have no subsequent testament to guide our interpretation?

I have studied how a number of theologians and preachers discuss the move from time-bound text to timeless theological truths.[65] I have noticed that a model that has not been as widely used or influential in hermeneutical circles as I think it should be is the process of Bible translation known as dynamic equivalence (or functional equivalence). The heart of dynamic equivalence translation theory is the attempt to create the same impact in the receptor language of those who are hearing the text now as was created in the original audience of the text. In order to do this, Eugene Nida and others have developed a complex model of translational theory.[66] I recognize that this theory has both shortcomings and strengths, and that it is the subject of considerable debate, in which I have been a participant. The intricacies of that debate are not my concern here, though I will say that virtually all debate over Bible translation theory today takes as its starting point Nida's dynamic equivalence, which tries to move from one language and context—an ancient and sacred one—to a modern language and context. My contention is that this is the task not only of translation, but also of theology itself, and that the procedure of one may well be essentially the procedure of the other.

I will try to summarize the theory. The notion is that one must first determine the kernel or heart of what is being said in the original text. In translation theory this is applied to the sentence, but I think that the notion can be and often is extended to larger units, including larger theological units. This requires a process

65. For example, W. C. Kaiser, *Toward an Exegetical Theology* (Grand Rapids: Baker, 1981); J. R. W. Stott, *Between Two Worlds: The Art of Preaching in the Twentieth Century* (Grand Rapids: Eerdmans, 1982); W. L. Liefeld, *New Testament Exposition: From Text to Sermon* (Grand Rapids: Zondervan, 1984).

66. Among many important works, the three essential ones are E. A. Nida, *Toward a Science of Translating, with Special Reference to Principles and Procedures Involved in Bible Translating* (Leiden: Brill, 1964); E. A. Nida and C. R. Taber, *The Theory and Practice of Translation* (Leiden: Brill, 1969); J. de Waard and E. A. Nida, *From One Language to Another: Functional Equivalence in Bible Translating* (Nashville: Nelson, 1986). For discussion of some issues, see S. E. Porter and R. S. Hess, eds., *Translating the Bible: Problems and Prospects* (Journal for the Study of the New Testament: Supplement Series 173; Sheffield: Sheffield Academic Press, 1999).

of differentiating the essential from the ephemeral, the enduring from the contingent, the pertinent from the impertinent. Then one must put this kernel into the equivalent form of expression in the receptor language—today's theological language—so that it has the same effect on the present receiver as it did on the first hearer. This framework no doubt begs a number of questions in terms of how we establish the original kernel, how much we know about the effect of the writing on the first audience, what latitude we have in creating the equivalent response, and so on. Nevertheless, I think that these questions are addressable and, even if not completely overcome, enlightening for understanding. Here we must draw upon the range of the best thinking and practice at our disposal in terms of biblical, cultural, historical, and linguistic study, without thinking that these particular models are a substitute for the theological task itself. Surely we have some idea of the meaning of the text of Scripture and of the response to the biblical text—if not the actual response,[67] at least the intended response that elicited the communication.[68] We may have to return to how we formulate our theology in each day and age, and with various receptor groups in mind, but that seems consistent with how the original gospel message was presented: within a context, but without losing its christological center.

In a distinct sense, though without wishing to equate the two in their entireties, I believe that an adequate basis for New Testament theological hermeneutics is the same framework that undergirds dynamic equivalence translational theory, since, after

67. In many instances we seem to have a good indication of the response—for example, in the responses in other Pauline letters, or even in the narrative as provided by the book of Acts. My position is that Acts provides a reliable account of the developments of early Christianity, including Paul's missionary journeys. On this, Professor Marshall and I most certainly agree. See Marshall, *Acts of the Apostles*, 83–97, and my *The Paul of Acts: Essays in Literary Criticism, Rhetoric, and Theology* (Wissenschaftliche Untersuchungen zum Neuen Testament 115; Tübingen: Mohr, 1999) (reprinted as *Paul in Acts* [Peabody, Mass.: Hendrickson, 2001]).

68. Hallidayan functional linguistics is concerned with determining the context of situation of a discourse. See S. E. Porter, "Dialect and Register in the Greek of the New Testament: Theory," in *Rethinking Contexts, Rereading Texts: Contributions from the Social Sciences to Biblical Interpretation* (ed. M. D. Carroll R.; Journal for the Study of the Old Testament: Supplement Series 299; Sheffield: Sheffield Academic Press, 2000), 190–208, esp. 198.

all is said and done, aren't we claiming that the Bible, rightly interpreted, is as relevant today as it was when it was written? If so, then the purpose of that text when it was written must be directly linked to the purpose that it has for us today, and the effect that it was intended to have then must be the effect that it should have on us today. Clearly, I have not fully worked out all of the implications of this hermeneutical/translational model for developing a contemporary theology, but it seems to me that the best sermons and the best theologies are trying to do what the best translations are trying to do: make God's Word come alive in our contemporary context in a way that speaks as meaningfully to our hearts as it did to the hearts of its first hearers.

Conclusion

I wish to say nothing that detracts from the fine work that many scholars have done in grappling with the modern hermeneutical dilemma, even if here I have not agreed with everything they have said. What I have offered, if it is worth anything, is not meant to point the finger at others and find their shortcomings, but rather to add to the discussion as we seek to advance our common understanding of the faith that binds us together. We must do so with our best theological tools at the ready. We must recognize the strengths and weaknesses of the methods that we are currently using. And, above all, we must be humble before the sacred text, whatever that might mean for our contemporary theological agenda.

Scripture Index

Subject Index